LOOSE HIM
and
LET HIM GO

BISHOP JOHN EKONG

authorHOUSE®

AuthorHouse™ UK
1663 Liberty Drive
Bloomington, IN 47403 USA
www.authorhouse.co.uk
Phone: 0800.197.4150

All Scriptural quotations are of King James Version of the Bible.

Published by AuthorHouse 07/22/2016

ISBN: 978-1-5246-3780-4 (sc)
ISBN: 978-1-5246-3779-8 (hc)
ISBN: 978-1-5246-3778-1 (e)

Contents

DEDICATION

This unique book is dedicated to God Almighty, whose inspiration and grace has made this work possible.

To my wife, Uwem, my children, Ediomo Abasi, Hossana, Precious and King David. They have been my joy and strength while on this work.

ACKNOWLEDGEMENT

My foremost thanks and appreciation go to the Almighty God for his love, favour and grace I receive everyday.

I am grateful to the following persons for their supports and encouragements; Engr/Deaconess A. Ikitde, Pastor Bassey William, Prince Jumbo, Pastor Richard, Pastor Ben Effiong, and all NACOM family.

Special thanks to my spiritual fathers for encouragement and strength: rev. Dr. Uma Ukpai, Arch Bishop Elijah Mboho, Dr. Morris Cerullo, San Diego, Bishop David Oyedepo, Bishop Mike Okonkwo, Arch Bishop Duncan William, and Apostle Dr. Isaiah Issong.

Thanks to Hon. Moses Essien, Hon. Umana Umana, and Elder Ubong Obot for their various supports and encouragements. May God bless and reward every one of them in Jesus name, Amen.

INTRODUCTION

The book, Loose Him and Let Him Go, is a unique revelation from God which deals deeply into the covenant roots and origins of lives, family and community. It's revelation is peculiar, it has never been written this way ever. The revelation is inspirational, and full of deliverance steps to full and total recovery. There is no area of demonic, ancestral and satanic covenants and curses that is not dealt with in a peculiar deliverance way. If a copy of this book enters your hand, just thank God because it takes you straight with power of the Holy Ghost borne through deep revelation into the realm of the spirit for complete and total freedom. It initiates you at instance into a new covenant with the Lordship of Jesus and opens a new and fantastic chapter for your life in a fulfilled way.

Beloved, believe God for this, your testimony will be great and specific by the time you read through this inspirational revelations.

Congratulations for a copy of this miracle and deliverance of rare value in your hand.

CHAPTER ONE

KNOWLEDGE OF THE WORD COMMANDS POWER

Heb 4:12-13

For the word of God is quick, and powerful, and sharper than any two-edged sword, piercing even to the dividing asunder of soul and spirit, and of the joints and marrow, and is a discerner of the thoughts and intents of the heart. Neither is there any creature that is not manifest in his sight: but all things are naked and opened unto the eyes of him with whom we have to do.

Life is a mystery. God from the beginning designs it to be so. Many people live their lives out without understanding the purpose for which they were created. To them, they are blinded to the truth of who they are. The revelation of our persons is in the knowledge of who God is.

God can only be revealed in his word. The word is spirit and life. The sovereign nature of God can only be optimized by the power of His word. The word speaks about whom he is, his power, his ability and his authority. The word discerns, seeing into the spirit, it exposes secrets and deep things of God. Whatever the word tells about God is true. The word is quick and powerful, breaking into the spirit of man. It discerns the thoughts. No secret is hid from Him; all things are naked and open to him. It tells the past, the present and the future. No one knows the spirit of man except by the spirit of God. We can only discover our nature, purpose and destiny by giving attendance to the word of God. It reveals your future before you walk into it. Jesus understood God's mission for his life as he read the word.

Luke 4:17-20

And there was delivered unto him the book of the prophet Esaias. And when he had opened the book, he found the place where it was written, The Spirit of the Lord is upon me, because he hath anointed me to preach the gospel to the poor; he hath sent me to heal the brokenhearted, to preach deliverance to the captives, and recovering of sight to the blind, to set at liberty them that are bruised, To preach the acceptable year of the Lord. And he closed the book, and he gave it again to the minister, and sat down. And the eyes of all them that were in the synagogue were fastened on him.

If you take a close summary of this scripture, you will agree with me that, Jesus saw, the mission, the purpose of his life on earth in these verses. No wonder, he was not fumbling, nor confused, rather He was very insightful, focused and very determined. He came to preach, to heal, deliver, set the captives free, and preach recovery, restoration, power and salvation. There were distractions here and there but this could not take his attention.

The people who enjoyed his ministry came to take him and to force him to be their king, he escape the trap because that was a distraction. Should men made him king and he consented to it; he would have lost his position divinely ordained as the king of kings. The true understanding that guided him to the fulfillment of his mission came when he opened the Book, he saw the definition of his mission in the book, written and sealed until he unlock the book, and read it for himself. Don't wait for one to tell you who you are, go to the book. Daniel said I understood by book what God's and purpose had been for his people Israel. The bible says as soon as Jesus read and had revelation of the father's mission on his life, he closed the book and began to Minister, and all eyes were on him. His fame was heard everywhere, the anointing came to fulfill the assignment. He had the father's backing, grace must multiply, favour increase, healing manifest, dead raised, souls saved, demons cast out, blinds receive their sight, the captives were delivered and God was with him. You need this spirit of revelation that discovers your purpose and destiny. It stirs up the giants and wakes up the champions. It quickens, enlightens the mind and loss the power and ability to perform.

John 6:63

It is the spirit that quickeneth; the flesh profiteth nothing: the words that I speak unto you, they are spirit, and they are life.

Until the spirit of God through the word of God reveals the purpose of God in your life, you will be lost in the crowd, ignorant is destiny destroyer. The scripture shows, the word is spirit and life. Until you are affected and impacted by the word of God, your spirit is dead and your destiny defeated; your life caged and your purpose stolen by the enemy called ignorant. For lack of knowledge my people are destroyed.

Jeremiah knew his life purpose beyond conception through the revelation of the word. The Lord challenged him out of self low esteem and inabilities. He told him clear who he was created to be. The Bible says:

3

Jer 1:4-7

Then the word of the Lord came unto me, saying, Before I formed thee in the belly I knew thee; and before thou camest forth out of the womb I sanctified thee, and I ordained thee a prophet unto the nations. Then said I, Ah, Lord God! behold, I cannot speak: for I am a child. But the Lord said unto me, Say not, I am a child: for thou shalt go to all that I shall send thee, and whatsoever I command thee thou shalt speak.

Here, we see: what Jeremiah knew about himself was quite contradictory to the purpose and plan of God concerning him. The Lord made him a prophet even before he was conceived, ordained and sanctified for a generational assignments but he had no idea about his profound mission. When God in his love and mercy revealed his purpose unto him, he saw himself absolutely unqualified for it. He said he is a child; he cannot speak. At that point you can see how he humiliated himself. You know at what age a child can speak. That is how undeveloped he felt he was.

It does not matter what inheritance the father had willed for his son, as long as he is a child, underdeveloped, immature, he has no knowledge nor authority or claim over the estate until he becomes a son, most of us Christians today are like that, children of God, not growing to the full knowledge of their son-ship in God nor able to comprehend the magnitude of wealth and inheritance God has willed unto us at regeneration. The devil is still toying with our lives, Jeremiah said I cannot speak.

Most Christians today cannot speak. Faith comes alive when we declare it; mountains are moved when we speak to it. Dead is raised back to life by our words, health released when the word is spoken. Things are created in the heavenlies when we speak. Burt Jeremiah said I cannot speak.

Life and death are in the power of the tongue. The eyes of God is his words, let's see how he sees:

2 Cor 4:13

It is written: "I believed; therefore I have spoken." With that same spirit of faith we also believe and therefore speak,

When you speak what you believe, God is activated, miracle is stirred, and potentials are quickened. Things are brought under control. Our authority is in our words.

Pharaoh said to Joseph rule us by your words, we are rulers when we are speakers, and we are commanders when we exercise authority of the word. You don't know a man until he speaks. Faith comes by hearing the word of God. The speaker is faith carrier. Without faith it is impossible to please God. We limit him and offend him when we don't believe him.

Mountains which are confrontational situations are revealed, destroyed, brought under control only when we exercise our words.

Mark 11:22-23

And Jesus answering saith unto them, Have faith in God. For verily I say unto you, That whosoever shall say unto this mountain, Be thou removed, and be thou cast into the sea; and shall not doubt in his heart, but shall believe that those things which he saith shall come to pass; he shall have whatsoever he saith.

This scripture starts with whosoever and ends with whatsoever. If whosoever, means any person, black or white, educated or uneducated, then whatsoever means anything, known or unknown, visible or invisible. This is the law that controls the release. You claim it when you proclaim it. If mountains literally were created by the spoken word of God, then by the word of God spoken in faith it can be removed. You challenge it if you want to change it. Isles are waiting for your law (word) life answers to what we declare. Life and death are in the power of the tongue. The word puts life in the world.

Heb 11:3

Through faith we understand that the worlds were framed by the word of God, so that things which are seen were not made of things which do appear.

The spoken word of God brings the living world we are in today. You can create your world by your word. But you have to understand the power of the word, speak in faith. Only the word of God spoken in faith can address the visible and invisible worlds bringing powers and authorities to the obedience of Christ. Exercise it and you will be called the Son of the Most High. Call those things that be not as though there were. Control the spirit world by your words.

The earnest expectation of all creature wait for the manifestation of the sons of men in the name of Jesus. It lies in the power of your words. Where the word of the king is there is power. Say it and see it, the eye sees what the mouth declares. The word is spirit. It is the breath of God. The invisible that controls the visible. What is not created in the spirit by faith is not manifesting in the natural. It is the word that birth the flesh.

John 1:14

And the Word was made flesh, and dwelt among us, (and we beheld his glory, the glory as of the only begotten of the Father,) full of grace and truth.

This scripture reveals the power of manifestation through the word. The word is made flesh. Destiny manifestation is the potential to call forth our future by the word of God. We can only experience so much that we can believe God for.

John 5:25

Verily, verily, I say unto you, The hour is coming, and now is, when the dead shall hear the voice of the Son of God: and they that hear shall live.

There are dead situations everywhere waiting the command of the sons of God. The voice of faith declares with authority. Jesus called Lazarus with a loud voice out of the grave and he commanded, loose him and let him go and he was loosed. This is what we missed when we watch things happening and we are not bold enough to speak. The bible says in Isaiah 17 vs. 45. According to the work of my hand command ye me, the exercise of authority over situations is in the level of knowledge possessed in the word of God. Jesus says if you don't doubt in your heat you will have it in your hands. We are dying while the word is living. You can see it tomorrow if you say it today. Jesus cursed the fig tree in Mark's Gospel when he was going to Bethany from Jerusalem and got the result the next day. Please read Mark 11 vs. 11-20. The bible says when they came back by it, they saw the fig free had withered from the root and Peter calling to remembrance the word of the lord a day before, said; Master the fig tree had withered so soon and Jesus answered and said, have faith in God. Our problem today is lack of faith. Inability to believe in the power of God working through us both by will and to do according to his divine purpose. We fear it might not happen if we say it. I don't want to dent my integrity, we protect who we are and value it far beyond whom God is to us.

We doubt God and what he puts in us. He said to Jeremiah see, I have put my word in thy mouth go and speak to these nations for I am

7

with you. It plays back on how we lack trust in one another. We lost our identity. Peter only call to remembrance when he saw it happen. May be he did not believe it could happen or happen so quickly.

The bible says the word is quick and powerful. Result comes when faith is revealed. The word fixes it immediately in the spirit and watch out for manifestation in the natural.

Beloved, we are talking about knowledge that commands power of freedom, miracle, healing and restoration.

God's blessing is released in the vessel of faith when faith is not exercised, blessing is not released.

Please look at this scripture and you will see faith at work.

2 Kings 6:6-7

And the man of God said, Where fell it? And he shewed him the place. And he cut down a stick, and cast it in thither; and the iron did swim. Therefore said he, Take it up to thee. And he put out his hand, and took it.

There are wonderful revelations shown here; the man of God said, where? This seeks to know the place. Sometimes we don't know the place where authority is needed to be exercised. When he knew the place he did something very foolishly by the assessment men. He cuts a stick and cast into the river. How do you expect stick to bring Iron, well I am exercising my faith in the word of God that says whatsoever you believe God for, you shall have it.

He believed that actions of faith stirs up the supernatural response and that with God nothing shall be impossible. The Lord reached upon his faith and made the Iron to swim, unbelievable miracle but it happened because somebody believed God for it. Please watch this, the lost iron is swimming right now, but the prophet said to the man who lost it: take it up. The prophet believed God and acted his faith by doing the unusual and caused the iron to swim, but the man who needed the iron also needed to exercise his hand of faith to pick it up.

Faith is the power that draws the Hand of God and causes the supernatural occurrence in the natural world. And the man of God said. We see it when we say it. Listen to God speak:-

Ezek 12:21-24,25

And the word of the Lord came unto me, saying, Son of man, what is that proverb that ye have in the land of Israel, saying, The days are prolonged, and every vision faileth? Tell them therefore, Thus saith the Lord God; I will make this proverb to cease, and they shall no more use it as a proverb in Israel; but say unto them, The days are at hand, and the effect of every vision. For I am the Lord: I will speak, and the word that I shall speak shall come to pass; it shall be no more prolonged: for in your days, O rebellious house, will I say the word, and will perform it, saith the Lord God.

All we have seen in this scripture is God's master plan which works through his word. He makes us to know things have changed. He acts speed on what he says; but the Land of Israel was still holding unto the ancient proverbs. God delays, perhaps, this might be the reason we are discourage to exercise our authority in the word over circumstances beyond our control. He says in your rebellious house (generation) will I speak a word and perform it. The supremacy of God is clearly displayed in creation by his word. And God said let there be; and it was so. Thank God.

Ps 107:20

He sent his word, and healed them, and delivered them from their destructions.

God's faithful messenger is his word, released in the spirit by faith has ability to heal and to deliver, you may ask, why are people still bound by bondage of sickness. We don't open up to the power of the word of God. God reaches us through his word; his word is life, spirit and light.

John 8:32

And ye shall know the truth, and the truth shall make you free.

Knowledge is power and power exercises, authority. Whatsoever you shall bind on earth is bound in heaven. Often times, we wait for heaven, whereas we are to activate heaven by our word. It takes the one who holds the key to unlock the door.

Jesus said to Peter and I quote:

Matt 16:19

And I will give unto thee the keys of the kingdom of heaven: and whatsoever thou shalt bind on earth shall be bound in heaven: and whatsoever thou shalt loose on earth shall be loosed in heaven.

The key to the kingdom of heaven is with us and not with God. He gave I after resurrection. So if you don't unlock heaven, you are gone. He says whatsoever we loose on earth is loosed in heaven. Our freedom is in our hands. Speak into the heavens, declare things and watch the power of the wicked dismantled and scattered. The keys to everything is with us. Stop blaming God, you open the door for him to come in and do whatever you want him to do. The centurion said speak the word only and my servant shall be healed. The unstoppable servant of God is the one who knows his authority and exercise it. The word is our weapon of warfare.

2 Cor 10:4-5

(For the weapons of our warfare are not carnal, but mighty through God to the pulling down of strong holds;) Casting down imaginations, and every high thing that exalteth itself against the knowledge of God, and bringing into captivity every thought to the obedience of Christ;

We have kept God outside our activity and life for to long. He said,

Rev 3:20

Behold, I stand at the door, and knock: if any man hear my voice, and open the door, I will come in to him, and will sup with him, and he with me.

The word is our power, weapon of warfare. Mighty things are pulled down without our sweats. Power surrender when we exercise it, demons are cast out by the word, dead raised, chains of bondage are loosed when we speak. Lazarus came back to life when Jesus spoke.

John 11:43-44

And when he thus had spoken, he cried with a loud voice, Lazarus, come forth. And he that was dead came forth, bound hand and foot with graveclothes: and his face was bound about with a napkin. Jesus saith unto them, Loose him, and let him go.

Lazarus had died and was buried four days before Jesus arrived. Humanly, it was believed his arrival was late, whatever he could have done, time had past, people were worried, murderers everywhere, sisters lost all hope. But Jesus walked in with a word I am the resurrection and the life, he that believes in me though he were dead shall live again. He told them to believe in God then, they would see the glory of God. It is difficult to exercise that faith in the face of such a hopeless situation. Sometimes, the case similar to this occurs to us and we do not know how to face it, our faith looks too small to face it, it is like the red sea, God would want us to face it for unprecedented miracle, it still happens today whenever we face it. It is like David stepping out to confront Goliath, all hope is lost, champions in war, doubted his victory but faith in God braved him up and he face it and brought victory to the army of the Lord.

God sometimes allows such challenges to face us to see how mature we are in our walk with him. Until Elisha threw a stick into the sea, the iron did not swim or until he acted, God did not react, He was silent over the situation. Only our faith action breaks God's silence and releases the supernatural power necessary for the miraculous. Let's finish the story: Jesus when he had thus spoken, he cried with a LOUD VOICE Lazarus come forth, you see, the voice stirred up the spirit realm loosing grip and power of dead upon a man who was buried for four days and he stood up bound, with grave cloths. Beloved we are living in the midst of people who are bound with grave clothes. Dead is hunting people everyday, veils of darkness have covered peoples' identity and destiny. We must rise to this challenge; the blood of Jesus has never lost his power.

You see here that every word Jesus spoke accomplish a mission, the first cry weakened him and he stood up bound, he had to give another command, loose him and let him go. Then the power of the second command loosed at the grave clothes and napkin u0pon his face.

The word shows that death is the terminator of destiny and that now he is back to life he must start his life allover again. At the command of the Lord his life picked up again, people were amazed upon what they saw. Jesus did these by demonstrating the power of the word of God. We can do likewise. He said greater works shall thou do because I go back to my father. This means, the authority to do more is with us. This scripture further strengthens us to sleep out and declare what we want to see.

Isa 55:11

So shall my word be that goeth forth out of my mouth: it shall not return unto me void, but it shall accomplish that which I please, and it shall prosper in the thing whereto I sent it.

Let's look at the key factors in this scripture "my word" this implies that if the word is part of my life, that is my authority and power, but it will make no effect if the second factor is not applied, which is "That goeth forth out of my mouth". This implies that you can only impact, create and perform when it is spoken. We have the mouth and the word. "It shall not return void". This is where our faith should be encouraged to speak knowing that it will bring a positive result. "It shall accomplish that which I please". The word accomplish is actualization and fulfillment. It prospers, it achieves mission. It does not fail. Our purpose in life will be fulfilled with great joy and excitement when we master the WORD.

The word is nigh unto thee even the word of life, even in thy mouth, s peak it and you will have life. The word is sprit and life. When you speak, it breaks every flame of fire and breaks even Cedar of Lebanon. That is, mighty things happen, doors open, breakthroughs and miracles are testified about, God is great, the word says so. Let the redeemed of the Lord say so, and see just that.

13

THE SWORD OF THE SPIRIT

Eph 6:16-17

Above all, taking the shield of faith, wherewith ye shall be able to quench all the fiery darts of the wicked. And take the helmet of salvation, and the sword of the Spirit, which is the word of God:

Life is warfare. Technology of today shows that nations which are feared are those equipped in high and sophisticated nuclear weapons. This is to get such nations prepared for war attacks. But God has also prepared onslaught on the devil. Our weapons are the shields of faith to quench all fiery attacks of the wicked. The helmet of salvation: once saved, you are saved and equipped to disarm and neutralize the forces of the wicked. The weapon is the sword of the spirit which is the word of God. When the word is activated by speaking, the sword is quickened in the spirit. The battle is spiritual; it takes the sword of the spirit to penetrate the strongholds of the wicked. If you don't have the word, you don't have the sword, the battle will be lost in the spirit world. The word is the dynamite of God in the spirit when the spirit is at work, you cannot stand the sword-Release the word, then the sword is activated in the spirit and victory is assured.

Prov 1:23

Turn you at my reproof: behold, I will pour out my spirit unto you, I will make known my words unto you.

The word of God corrects our lives and puts us on the reach of the spirit of God. The spirit touches those who are changed by the word. The spirit interprets the word of God. Revelation comes to make the word alive. Our lives can only refresh and impact our generation by the spirit out pour. Rain refreshes and causes germination which grows into fruition and harvest.

Ezek 37:4

Again he said unto me, Prophesy upon these bones, and say unto them, O ye dry bones, hear the word of the Lord.

Until the word was received the breath of life (spirit of life) did not enter, no movement of bones, no shaking was noticed. The word that I speak, there are spirit and there life. The word says it but the spirit produces it. God is only committed to do what his word says. Our healing, deliverance and prosperity lie in the power of our tongue. Loose him and let him go. The man Lazarus was set free immediately.

AUTHORITY IN THE NAME OF JESUS

Prov 18:10

The name of the Lord is a strong tower: the righteous runneth into it, and is safe.

Right in the Old Testament, the authority in the name of the Lord had been licenced. A strong tower, a tower is a height, a lofty structure raised above all, it serves as a place of safety, Lot requested to run the mountain top from the flame of Sodom and Gomorrah. You see above all when you are on a tower. The descendants of Noah were building tower of Babel for their safety against the next flood of danger. It's a place of defence.

There is more to it when we use the name of the Lord as a strong tower, righteous runs to it. This means that we have a place to run to when danger pursues. It is our city of refuge from storms of life, from onslaught of the wicked. Also, it is the place of victory and solace for the redeemed of the Lord, our shelter in the heat and storms of life. The only name that draws a line against what pursues us is the name of The Lord. And once you identify with the name you are saved and safe.

Acts 4:12

Neither is there salvation in any other: for there is none other name under heaven given among men, whereby we must be saved.

This name is a gift to the redeemed, our salvation, healing, deliverance and restoration come through this name. The whole heaven and earth bow at the mention of this name.

By the authority in the name of Jesus I declare your healing, deliverance, and breakthrough and command every demon and their strongholds to be broken. I exercise the power of that name for your instant miracle in Jesus name. Thank God how for your testimonies.

At the name of Jesus demon trembles, their authority behind powers and principalities crumble to the foundations. Jesus is LORD forever. The high priests, Sadducees and captains of the temple wondered.

Acts 4:16-17

Saying, What shall we do to these men? for that indeed a notable miracle hath been done by them is manifest to all them that dwell in Jerusalem; and we cannot deny it. But that it spread no further among the people, let us straitly threaten them, that they speak henceforth to no man in this name.

The thread posed upon the apostles by high priests, Sadducees and the Pharisees was to stop the speaking in the name of Jesus. The more they speak in that name, the more miracles spread. They wanted to stop the spread by stopping the speaking in that name. Our brand name for notable miracle is Jesus. That is the heritage we have from the Lord. In the name of Jesus of Nazareth rise up and walk, Peter said it and immediately, the cripple man rose up and walked into the temple.

What manner of man is Jesus that even the wind and the wave obeyed him. Salvation is received in this name, healing is received in this name. dead raised in this name, baptism in the spirit is received in this name. Power to overcome sin and devil is received in this name. We are made whole when faith is exercised in this name.

Acts 3:16

And his name through faith in his name hath made this man strong, whom ye see and know: yea, the faith which is by him hath given him this perfect soundness in the presence of you all.

Acts 4:10

Be it known unto you all, and to all the people of Israel, that by the name of Jesus Christ of Nazareth, whom ye crucified, whom God raised from the dead, even by him doth this man stand here before you whole.

You can be the man of the woman today standing up with your miracle or healing of any kind. All you need is exercise of faith in the name of Jesus. Heaven and Earth with all their hosts were summoned by God, the father to act in submission to that name.

Phil 2:8-13

And being found in fashion as a man, he humbled himself, and became obedient unto death, even the death of the cross. Wherefore God also hath highly exalted him, and given him a name which is above every name: That at the name of Jesus every knee should bow, of things in heaven, and things in earth, and things under the earth; And that every tongue should confess that Jesus Christ is Lord, to the glory of God the Father. Wherefore, my beloved, as ye have always obeyed, not as in my presence only, but now much more in my absence, work out your own salvation with fear and trembling. For it is God which worketh in you both to will and to do of his good pleasure.

The name of Jesus is above all other names. Every name bows to this name. His humility and obedience to the will of the father has exalted him with this name. Demons tremble at this name. Whatever name situation you are going through might clam, in Jesus name there are bound forever.

Doctors might give name or names to your sickness or diseases to scare you. Their inability to handle such situation might put fear of death in you but the Bible says, this man through faith in the name of Jesus stand before you whole or healed. All you need is faith in the name of Jesus and rebuke the demons and take authority in this name and in the blood of Jesus against them, they will bow and cry out. Jesus cast out devils with his words. Psalms 107 vs. 20: says: Ps 107:20

He sent his word, and healed them, and delivered them from their destructions. Whatever you bind on earth is bound in heaven and what you loose on earth is loosed in heaven. This is our power of attorney; use it and live big in freedom and power.

AUTHORITY IN THE BLOOD OF JESUS

As believers, we have to understand the power and authority released in the blood of Jesus. God has not sent us to battle without weapons, we have seen the power in the word of God, the name of Jesus, and all these are the weapons God has equipped us with intending for us to always be on the winning lists.

Beloved, the blood of Jesus has not only cleansed and washed away our sins it was offered as the final requirement to satisfy the father's demand for sin; for total freedom, legality and seal of power and authority over every power, kingdoms and dominion. The price has been fully paid. You have right before God, and authority in his blood against all activities of the devil.

In my other book, "Blood is the Final", it shows that once the blood is shed, the case is settled. Literally once the blood is shed, life is gone for whatever purpose.

Here, the purpose of the blood of Jesus was for our total cleansing and total emancipation from sin and its consequences.

Lev 17:6

And the priest shall sprinkle the blood upon the altar of the Lord at the door of the tabernacle of the congregation, and burn the fat for a sweet savour unto the Lord.

Right from the Old Testament time, blood was treated as sacred and could only be handled by the priests with strict instructions. It settled sin consequences of men once shed. This was pointing to something that was to come, Jesus our sacrificial Lamb.

The bible says, when the priests will offer it, and sprinkle the blood upon the altar and the door of the tabernacle of congregation the LORD received it as a sweet savor. It typifies something very deep. When people violate the statute and commandment of the LORD, the LORD was wroth with them, death could occur in the tabernacle but when the priest shed blood for such sin, the LORD smells sweet savor it means the wrath was over, the blood reconciled, God was in harmony again with them. Under the law life was constantly preserved by blood atonement over sins. Man was not allowed to eat blood; it is sacred life and God's gift, pointing to Jesus, the gift of life to humanity through his blood.

Lev 17:11

For the life of the flesh is in the blood: and I have given it to you upon the altar to make an atonement for your souls: for it is the blood that maketh an atonement for the soul.

The only acceptable divine currency for the settlement of man's sinful penalty is the blood of the innocent Lamb. And when atonement is made upon the altar for sins, God is settled and reconciliation is made. The blood of animal could not satisfy this demand forever. But God accepted it pointing unto the final price that will be paid through the blood of Jesus once and for all.

Heb 9:7-12

But into the second went the high priest alone once every year, not without blood, which he offered for himself, and for the errors of the people: The Holy Ghost this signifying, that the way into the holiest of all was not yet made manifest, while as the first tabernacle was yet standing: Which was a figure for the time then present, in which were offered both gifts and sacrifices, that could not make him that did the service perfect, as pertaining to the conscience; Which stood only in meats and drinks, and divers washings, and carnal ordinances, imposed on them until the time of reformation. But Christ being come an high priest of good things to come, by a greater and more perfect tabernacle, not made with hands, that is to say, not of this building; Neither by the blood of goats and calves, but by his own blood he entered in once into the holy place, having obtained eternal redemption for us.

The passage is quoted at its length to show you how the eternal price of our redemption had been paid by Jesus Christ, through his shed blood on Calvary. NO other sacrifice is necessary, his blood serves eternal purpose for our salvation, reconciliation, restoration, and puts us back to our place of power, authority and inheritance. Praise God.

Eph 4:30

And grieve not the holy Spirit of God, whereby ye are sealed unto the day of redemption.

Jesus, through eternal spirit shed his blood once and for all and seals our lives for eternal salvation. Understand me, the blood satisfies the father's demand eternally but our salvation, depends on our relationship with God and the receiving of the cleansing through this blood to serve God with a right conscience toward God and man, not accepting or indulging in any other sacrifice but through this precious blood of Jesus, our lives are purchased, we are no longer living for ourselves.

1 Cor 6:19-20

Do you not know that your body is a temple of the Holy Spirit, who is in you, whom you have received from God? You are not your own; you were bought at a price. Therefore honor God with your body.

You see, as soon as this blood price was paid, our lives worth went up, no more vagabond, no more illegitimate, no more slaves, but God's property, God's temple, God's habitation, the home of God. The devil cannot mess the Lord's House, The spirit of the Lord dwells in us. Praise God. Don't ask me of myself. I'm not my own, God answers every bargain on my life because through the blood of Jesus, I am now bought and owned by him. If you want to see me, see him, if you want to sell me, buy from his hands, I'm now God's property. I have eternal value. My worth is the price paid, the priceless price of the eternal blood of Jesus. The values of products are the price on it. God is now a waster; he knows what I mean for him before he spends his life to get mine. The devil can not reach me without him.

Col 3:3-4

For ye are dead, and your life is hid with Christ in God. When Christ, who is our life, shall appear, then shall ye also appear with him in glory.

This is a very important scripture to me. He controls my life; my life is hid in him, when you get him, that's me for you.

If the enemy kills him the second time, I am gone because my life is hid in him and I was dead in him. When he appears, you see me. When he disappears, I am gone. This is a mystery. You can't catch me without him. In him I live and move and have my being, so says the Bible in Acts of the Apostle Chapter seventeen verse twenty-eight. I am his offspring and no one can use me for offering without his knowledge. I am complete in him.

PROPHETIC CONFESSION AND PRAYER

If these mysteries are acknowledged by you, say this PRAYER with me:

Lord Jesus, I receive you into my life as my personal Lord and Saviour. Thank you for washing away my sins through your blood shed on the cross of Calvary. I now stand for given Amen.

Therefore I take authority in the name and the blood of Jesus over every force of darkness, sickness, disease, and demonic covenants or curses upon my life and family. I command them to loose their grips over my life in Jesus name. I declare the curse of covenant broken. I receive healing, deliverance in my body, salvation to my soul; I declare every covenant of soul tie broken in Jesus name Amen. I command my soul out of any trap of the devil in Jesus name. I also denounce every evil covenant of practice perpetrated by my forbearers who have claim over my life, family and my future in Jesus name. I receive my freedom, restoration and total cleansing now through the blood of Jesus. Whatever was done against me consciously or unconsciously I denounce them and by application of the blood of Jesus I redeem my soul. I shall not die. I disappear from the kingdom of darkness with all my tokens; the spell of witchcraft over me is broken and destroyed. I am redeemed from the family curse, death and barrenness through the blood of his blood on the cross. I announce my freedom officially through the resurrection power of Jesus. I am free, I know it.

> *John 8:32,36*
>
> *And ye shall know the truth, and the truth shall make you free.*
>
> *If the Son therefore shall make you free, ye shall be free indeed.*

I feel good now. Let's read on.

CHAPTER TWO

BREAKING THE COVENANT OF DESOLATION

COVENANTS AND THE EFFECTS

Many things that happen to individuals today are as a result of certain covenants and vows which were made many years ago. Most routes our destiny travels through over ages are founded by covenants entered. Even our salvation today, through Jesus Christ is a product of the covenant that God entered with Abraham thousands of years ago.

A covenant is defined as a formal agreement between two or more persons that is legally binding. It is a mutual agreement that one gets into which affects ones course of life. There is always a spirit behind every covenant to effect actions on the term of such covenant. From the above definition, it implies that a covenant is not a mere request; it is not a promise or a vow. It is not a decree or a command to be observed. It is an agreement that involves at least two parties. Before any covenant is established, the parties involved must agree on a term upon which they are bonded.

1 Sam 18:3-4

Then Jonathan and David made a covenant, because he loved him as his own soul. And Jonathan stripped himself of the robe that was upon him, and gave it to David, and his garments, even to his sword, and to his bow, and to his girdle.

Here, we have seen Jonathan and David entering into a covenant with exchange of personal belongings to validate the consent of both parties. There must be a property upon which the covenant is founded; I call it covenant token for the purpose of registering consent. Here Jonathan gave his robe, his garments, his sword, his bow and his girdle to David to seal the covenant. In the later chapters, we will understand more about covenant token. A covenant may be suggested by one party, yet the other must convincingly agree before it is established.

Gen 31:43-44, 51-52.

And Laban answered and said unto Jacob, These daughters are my daughters, and these children are my children, and these cattle are my cattle, and all that thou seest is mine: and what can I do this day unto these my daughters, or unto their children which they have born? Now therefore come thou, let us make a covenant, I and thou; and let it be for a witness between me and thee.

And Laban said to Jacob, Behold this heap, and behold this pillar, which I have cast betwixt me and thee; This heap be witness, and this pillar be witness, that I will not pass over this heap to thee, and that thou shalt not pass over this heap and this pillar unto me, for harm.

Here we see Laban tricking Jacob to enter into a covenant with him to dispossess Jacob of all his labored possessions.

The daughters he was referring to are Leah and Rachel which Jacob had duly worked for and married. The father Laban did not release them spiritually unto Jacob and the children were all Jacob's children, the cattle and everything were Jacobs's possessions, but Laban wanting to dispossess them from Jacob tricked him into a covenant of claim. He invited Jacob and said let us make a covenant between me and you. The claim of the covenant is not about Jacob but Jacob's possessions. Most of the covenants our forbearers entered are hunting after us, to claim and dispossess us of our rights, a spirit husband (marmaid spirit) is hunting a young woman in marriage or she is seeing herself in the water or having a defiling affairs in dreams with a demon in human nature, claiming, that she is his wife based on the term of covenant which defined the ownership of the descendants of such family. Until the tie is broken the spell will be binding.

> *Josh 24:22-25*
>
> *And Joshua said unto the people, Ye are witnesses against yourselves that ye have chosen you the Lord, to serve him. And they said, We are witnesses. Now therefore put away, said he, the strange gods which are among you, and incline your heart unto the Lord God of Israel. And the people said unto Joshua, The Lord our God will we serve, and his voice will we obey. So Joshua made a covenant with the people that day, and set them a statute and an ordinance in Shechem.*

Joshua took their words and vows to serve a living God and established into a covenant that binds them. Breaking it will be a violation with damaging consequences. Note it is very easy to enter into a covenant without minding the consequence, but to break it will take the grace and anointing of God.

Covenant wither with God or with devil don't just happen, there are made, you will understand how; as you read carefully down.

PROPERTIES OF COVENANT

There are certain things that are involved in the making of a meaningful and effective covenant. For any agreement to be a covenant, it must possess these properties, whether covenant with men, God or Satan.

(a) A COVENANT must have a TERM

The first step in establishing a covenant is to define the term. A TERM of covenant is the statement of the agreement clearly spelt out specifically (Matthew 12 vs. 37). The scope and the strength of such covenant are in the term. The working force is to actualize the term. It determines the benefit to the obedience and the consequence on defaulters and descendant travel line of the covenant. This is who in the generational line must be affected.

In God's covenant with Abram in Genesis 17, God clearly spelt out the term of agreement. This term shares the mutual benefits, the trapping persuasions.

> *Gen 17:1-6*
>
> *And when Abram was ninety years old and nine, the Lord appeared to Abram, and said unto him, I am the Almighty God; walk before me, and be thou perfect. And I will make my covenant between me and thee, and will multiply thee exceedingly. And Abram fell on his face: and God talked with him, saying, As for me, behold, my covenant is with thee, and thou shalt be a*

father of many nations. Neither shall thy name any
more be called Abram, but thy name shall be Abraham;
for a father of many nations have I made thee. And
I will make thee exceeding fruitful, and I will make
nations of thee, and kings shall come out of thee.

The unique definition of the terms is very appealing. The foundation of the covenant was laid on perfection, purity and sanctity of heart. This is the strength and the altar upon which this God's covenant is built, if Abraham must enjoy the benefit, he must observe the foundation upon which the term is defined.

God started by saying I will MAKE my covenant with thee. God's covenant when kept reveals blessing. Here the blessings are enormous. He promised to multiply and make him exceedingly fruitful. It brings increase and great fortune. He promised to make him a father of many nations - the originator of kings and dominion. To seal the sacredness of this covenant, he changed his name from Abram to Abraham. The secret of any covenant is in the secret names the partakers receive to keep the identity valid and sealed. Covenant with Satan at all levels; witchcraft and occult initiations are all founded on this secret to keep their performing identity hidden. You may not understand d that the biological name of any agents of darkness is not used once initiated, for example: if the person's name is known and addressed as Lucky, once initiated in either witchcraft or any other secret cult will have his initiation name. Lucky may be known in the spirit world of darkness and wickedness as mad dog. This is to protect his identity at the field of wicked activity. He may kill and kill, if caught and caused to swear to an oath (affidavit) native name "mbiam". This could kill if sworn deceitfully, but as long as people don't know his secret name (mad dog) with which the havoc was perpetuated, he may be forced to swear by Lucky but the actual spirit man behind the killing is mad dog. He may swear by Lucky and the terminal period expires and nothing happens to him, he could be set free that it was mere allegation. The secret is in the action name mad dog that is not known.

A change of name with understanding can also alter the evil trap set against you with your initial name. God also change Sarai's name to Sarah, a mother of many nations and her barrenness was broken and she bore Isaac. Laban entered into a covenant with Jacob on his way back from Haran, a covenant of heap that places a limitation on him for further advances. This was desolation that would frustrate all the plans and purposes of God for his life. But thank God, after the wrestling with the angel of the Lord, his name changed to Israel, whereby making the covenant of Laban with Jacob to be invalid. God works this way to redeem. Every covenant of barrenness and desolation made against you and your family, at the new birth with Jesus your name is changed into God's family, that negative covenant is broken and is made of non effect in Jesus name.

Between Abraham and Abemelech, the covenant term was also clearly defined.

Gen 21:30

And he said, For these seven ewe lambs shalt thou take of my hand, that they may be a witness unto me, that I have digged this well.

The conduct of action serves as a witness, a testimony of facts. It is clearly seen here that the effectiveness of any covenant is in the definition of the terms. These are words used by the one suggesting the covenant to attract the interest of, the other party to accept the entry.

(b) COVENANT MUST HAVE TOKENS

The tokens of covenant refer to the sing, evidence of guarantee for the establishment of the covenant. There can never be a covenant without a token from both parties which serves a seal of covenant. A token must be something tangible produced by those parties whether conscious or unconscious. The token could be your blood, nail cut, saliva, haircut, and money, material of any kind, food, signature, name, certificate, drinks, marriage materials, and clothes or after birth naval. The token once provided, represents your part in the covenant.

For instance, a naval taken after birth of a child and buried under a palm tree or plantain tree is a token establishing extension of the ancestral family covenant on that child, resulting in many complications as the child grows up, e.g. Eating in dreams, marriage or sex in dreams, bearing children in dreams, cobwebs spell, barrenness in real life, seeing oneself in water, or seeing oneself with snakes in dreams, poverty and all misfortune connected to the initiation of that child to the ancestral spell of the family. His presence though unconscious is being registered.

The spirit controlling the activity of the family now extends the cord of operations on his life. These are demonic and satanic yoke of bondage. It is a trap of fortune and destiny.

Gen 31:45-46, 48, 51-52.

And Jacob took a stone, and set it up for a pillar. And Jacob said unto his brethren, Gather stones; and they took stones, and made an heap: and they did eat there upon the heap. And Laban said,

This heap is a witness between me and thee this day. Therefore was the name of it called Galeed;

And Laban said to Jacob, Behold this heap, and behold this pillar, which I have cast betwixt me and thee; This heap be witness, and this pillar be witness, that I will not pass over this heap to thee, and that thou shalt not pass over this heap and this pillar unto me, for harm.

It is evidently clear what a token stands for in a specific covenant, a witness and a watch, Laban said the heap and the pillar will watch over us when we are absent from one and the other. It sets a watch. There is always a watching eye of the spirit after the covenant token is satisfied. He said when we are absent. Meaning even at death the covenant watch is still alive, so many things we go through in life today are the product of what our forbearers did and died, hunting and trailing after us, abusing our potentials and destiny, thank God for this book, the way out is real. Jesus is the way out:

In the case of Abraham's covenant with God, Tokens were involved.

Gen 17:11-14

And ye shall circumcise the flesh of your foreskin; and it shall be a token of the covenant betwixt me and you. And he that is eight days old shall be circumcised among you, every man child in your generations, he that is born in the house, or bought with money of any stranger, which is not of thy seed. He that is born in thy house, and he that is bought with thy money, must needs be circumcised: and my covenant shall be in your flesh for an everlasting covenant. And the uncircumcised man child whose flesh of his foreskin is not circumcised, that soul shall be cut off from his people; he hath broken my covenant.

This act of circumcision was the token of covenant which Abraham must keep if the covenant was to be established. God's part was a type pointing in shadow to a better covenant.

> *Gen 15:9-10, 18*
>
> *And he said unto him, Take me an heifer of three years old, and a she goat of three years old, and a ram of three years old, and a turtledove, and a young pigeon. And he took unto him all these, and divided them in the midst, and laid each piece one against another: but the birds divided he not.*
>
> *In the same day the Lord made a covenant with Abram, saying, Unto thy seed have I given this land, from the river of Egypt unto the great river, the river Euphrates:*

This is God's part of the covenant; blood was involved to seal the sacred ordinance with Abraham.

God told Noah after the blood in a covenant statement and said: This is the token of the covenant which I make between me and you and every living creature that is with you for perpetual generations. I do set my bow in the cloud, and it shall be for a Token of a covenant between me and the earth.

> *Gen 9:14-15*
>
> *And it shall come to pass, when I bring a cloud over the earth, that the bow shall be seen in the cloud: And I will remember my covenant, which is between me and you and every living creature of all flesh; and the waters shall no more become a flood to destroy all flesh.*

Here God's token of covenant was the bow in the cloud to serve as a reminder of his covenant commitment to Noah and the earth that He will no longer bring flood to destroy. This clearly shows the essentiality of token in every covenant to serve as a reminder, witness or mediator, establishing the registry of consents and commitments of the parties involved.

(c) COVENANT MUST HAVE A TARGET

The target of a covenant is the specific thing or things that are aimed to be accomplished through the covenant. It speaks of the ultimate goal of the covenant. What it seeks to achieve. It is the term that determines the target. The spirit behind such covenant works to fulfill the targets. If the covenant is satanic and the term define that a young man or woman should not marry or should be killed or should suffer some set backs and misfortunes in life, the demons on assignments will work to fulfill the targets, monitor him through crystal window, trail him in every area, cause misfortune here and there, marriage bad lucks, and miscarriages, broken engagements and death traps. In the case of God, it works to bring blessings, fruitfulness, favor and prosperity with peace and longevity of life. Some covenants are often named after the targets. For instance, if a covenant of peace is entered into, it is called covenant of peace.

Num 25:12-13

Wherefore say, Behold, I give unto him my covenant of peace: And he shall have it, and his seed after him, even the covenant of an everlasting priesthood; because he was zealous for his God, and made an atonement for the children of Israel.

Isa 54:10

For the mountains shall depart, and the hills be removed; but my kindness shall not depart from thee, neither shall the covenant of my peace be removed, saith the Lord that hath mercy on thee.

If the covenant is towards fruitfulness and increase, it is called covenant of increase if it is towards taking away life, it is called covenant of death.

(Joshua 6 vs. 26)

This was covenant of death placed on Jericho upon whosoever will rebuild it after God had destroyed it through Joshua. After many generations someone ignorant became a victim.

1 Kings 16:34

In Ahab's time, Hiel of Bethel rebuilt Jericho. He laid its foundations at the cost of his firstborn son Abiram, and he set up its gates at the cost of his youngest son Segub, in accordance with the word of the Lord spoken by Joshua son of Nun.

This Bethelite, ignorant of the covenant foundation went to build Jericho; he lost his two sons according to the word of the Lord through Joshua. Most people are suffering from the covenant statements made which they had no idea. Thank God, in Jesus Christ there is always a way out.

REMEDY

This is God's provision for solution. Prophetic Anointing deals with this type of covenant strongholds and reverse its consequence.

> *2 Kings 2:15*
>
> *And when the sons of the prophets which were to view at Jericho saw him, they said, The spirit of Elijah doth rest on Elisha. And they came to meet him, and bowed themselves to the ground before him.*
>
> *19-22*
>
> *And the men of the city said unto Elisha, Behold, I pray thee, the situation of this city is pleasant, as my lord seeth: but the water is naught, and the ground barren. And he said, Bring me a new cruse, and put salt therein. And they brought it to him. And he went forth unto the spring of the waters, and cast the salt in there, and said, Thus saith the Lord, I have healed these waters; there shall not be from thence any more death or barren land. So the waters were healed unto this day, according to the saying of Elisha which he spake.*

As soon as a double portion of Elijah's anointing fell on Elisha, the people of the city of Jericho moved to him and laid their situations before him and believed God for a healing miracle and the Lord did, today by the apostolic and prophetic mantle upon my life, every curse of death and barrenness in your life is declared broken in Jesus name. You are free to be fruitful and prosper. There is longevity of life to you and every member of the family. The covenant of death is broken.

In God's covenant with Abraham, the target was to make him a father to all generations and to make him fruitful in every endeavour.

(d) PROPHETIC PRAYER/CONFESSION

In the name of Jesus Christ, I take authority through the blood of Jesus over every covenant entered against me, known or unknown of such covenant to be uprooted, every term, target and token of such covenant that register my consent into it, by the token of the blood of Jesus, I destroy their tokens, I frustrate their efforts. I command the demons behind every covenant cast out. I invoke the power of the word of God as the sword of the spirit to break every tie, monitoring window and satanic spell over my life, family and business broken in Jesus name. I prophesy my soul fee, delivered from the strongholds of witchcraft in Jesus name. Oh my soul I speak authority unto you, you are redeemed with the blood of Jesus. Your shattered dreams are built back. The spell of bad luck is broken. By the sprinkling of the blood of Jesus over my soul and speaking of the same blood, I step out of the grave of frustration and desolation in Jesus name (Amen).

CHAPTER THREE

VOWS

A vow is a solemn promise, pledge or undertaking which one makes and becomes committed to. A vow is an oath sworn which becomes binding.

Num 30:2

> *If a man vow a vow unto the Lord, or swear an oath to bind his soul with a bond; he shall not break his word, he shall do according to all that proceedeth out of his mouth.*

It binds the soul; the word of a vow is a tie to the soul.

Vow is closely related to covenant. Every vow which binds is a covenant. A vow may have a term, which refers to the statement of the promise or oath or pledge, clearly and specifically defined. Jacob clearly stated out his vow in specific terms.

Gen 28:20-22

> *And Jacob vowed a vow, saying, If God will be with me, and will keep me in this way that I go, and will give me bread to eat, and raiment to put on, So that I come again to my father's house in peace; then shall the*

Lord be my God: And this stone, which I have set for a pillar, shall be God's house: and of all that thou shalt give me I will surely give the tenth unto thee.

God became interested in his mission because the term of his vow was defined in his favour. He promised to serve him alone, to build him a sanctuary and to pay the tenth part of every increase unto the Lord. So the Lord ratified the oath and worked with him to support and fight for him because he is a stake holder in his life and fortune.

Hannah vowed a vow unto the Lord and clearly defined her terms.

1 Sam 1:11

And she vowed a vow, and said, O Lord of hosts, if thou wilt indeed look on the affliction of thine handmaid, and remember me, and not forget thine handmaid, but wilt give unto thine handmaid a man child, then I will give him unto the Lord all the days of his life, and there shall no razor come upon his head.

Her commitment defined in the term of her vow, won the miraculous power of the Lord into her affliction and her barrenness was broken immediately. She clearly defined the owner of her gift. He will be dedicated unto the lord, a Nazarite, fully devoted unto the service of the Lord all the days of his life. The Lord stepped in because of interest. Often times, we refuse to commit ourselves to God in this kind of vows because we doubt our faithfulness in redemption. It is very impotent to know that when it is entered into in a right way, it pulls the strength of heaven into activity and suspends instantly every onslaught of the enemy.

Jephthah vowed a vow unto the Lord and clearly defined the term and it became binding.

Judg 11:30-31

And Jephthah vowed a vow unto the Lord, and said, If thou shalt without fail deliver the children of Ammon into mine hands, Then it shall be, that whatsoever cometh forth of the doors of my house to meet me, when I return in peace from the children of Ammon, shall surely be the Lord's, and I will offer it up for a burnt offering.

Jephthah brought God into the battle with the Ammonites in the term of his vow and God showed up for his victory. On a very hopeless life experience, your vow can commit and command God's divine intervention to reverse the situation but like I said earlier, we are not sincere to our commitment with the Lord always. The Bible says in

Eccl 5:4-6

When thou vowest a vow unto God, defer not to pay it; for he hath no pleasure in fools: pay that which thou hast vowed. Better is it that thou shouldest not vow, than that thou shouldest vow and not pay. Suffer not thy mouth to cause thy flesh to sin; neither say thou before the angel, that it was an error: wherefore should God be angry at thy voice, and destroy the work of thine hands?

The same way vows work with God to bring his blessing and supernatural involvement to work it out for us is the way vows made to Satan works, it releases at instance the spirit or demon to work, tie our souls to eternal damnation and slavery. Control our lives and destines. Bring curses and setbacks on our efforts, operates under a spell of monitoring spirit a widow is opened to our lives for Satan to view our dreams and activities, we are now under siege. Marriage vows broken carelessly bring sorrow and setbacks in marriage and Satan's accusations.

The oath of office taken on the swearing in the official office when broken by unfaithful dealing brings a curse on our lives and possessions. Vows made to a business partner when broken bring sorrows in the days ahead. The Bible portion we read in Ecclesiastes five says: suffer not your mouth to cause your flesh to sin. It attracts Gods anger and invokes the spirit of destruction on your endeavours. But by the blood of Jesus every vow we have entered with the devil consciously or unconsciously is declared broken today. Our souls are untied from such yokes in Jesus name.

Please note this; a vow may not necessarily involve another party. In situations where it does, the consent of the second party may not necessarily be sought before it is made, but rather be invited in the definition of the term of such vows. A vow may not always involve a token; instead, a pledge is often made which is usually redeemable at the accomplishment of such vows. Fulfilling the vow pledge is what the scripture in Job 22 vs. 27 refers to as paying of views. When vows are added to our prayer, it speeds up divine response.

A vow can be conditional or unconditional. A conditional vow is the one whose redemption or fulfillment is anchored on the accomplishment of a particular task. Examples of conditional vows include;

1. Jacob vow at Bethel genesis 28 vs. 20-22
2. Hannah's vow at Shiloh 1 Samuel 1 vs. 11
3. Jephthah's vow Judges 11 vs. 33,31.

In all these, pledges are made, Jacob pledged on Tenth of his increase, and building a temple, Hannah pledged giving the child unto God as a priest and a Nazarite. Jephthah pledged whatsoever will come out of his house to meet him after victory over the Ammonites to be given to the Lord as a burnt offering.

In unconditional vow, a pledge is made without any conditional term. Examples are the Levitical vow; our vow of service unto the Lord at new birth. God's unconditional love unto us is a good example.

Just as one can make a covenant with men, God or Satan, one can also make a vow to men, God or Satan, but the term defines the stand. If you make a vow unto the Lord, redeem it to release a blessing upon your life and destiny.

THE CONSEQUENCES OF BROKEN VOWS.

Vows as already defined earlier, are solemn promises pledges, undertaking or oaths sworn to which becomes binding. The trust, the confidence of undertaking the treaty by the partners involved lies in the bond sworn to. It keeps the flow of trust with those engaged there to and will grow the institutions, partners or the relationship in the case with God and opens us to abundant blessing when we honor our terms.

The consequences of breaking it could be very grievous and could mar all possible progress associated with such dealings.

In the case of broken vows with God, it invokes curses, brings limitation to the flow of blessings. It causes broken fellowship which could lead to loss of life fortunes. Similar is the consequences of broken vows with man or corporate existence as it halts relationship and retards progress and continuity.

Solution:

The word of God sets the precedent for all human challenges in life. Recovering process begins with repentance, confession of one's deeds, fault, to God or parties involved. Seeking a mediatory, reconciliatory counseling process that will lead to forgiveness and restoration. God forgives and restores. Prayer of repentance breaks the yokes and restores grace to God's glory.

CHAPTER FOUR

CURSES AND ITS EFFECTS

Curses are the invisible forces working against our lives and destiny. The force behind, bad-luck, frustration, barrenness and terminal sickness and poverty: the power of negativity and Satanity. It is the cord of affliction, sorrow and desolation.

Ancestral covenant which our forbearers entered into with spirits and ancient deities evoke a curse. Sacrifice to foul spirit in the air or water spirits bring curses upon the descendants of such perpetuator. Deliberately violation of divine ordinances without repentant will attract a curse. Robbing one of his legitimate rights or averting the right of innocence is a curse. Denying God of his divine institutionalized dues such like tithes and offerings bring a curse both on individuals and nations.

Mal 3:9-11

Ye are cursed with a curse: for ye have robbed me, even this whole nation. Bring ye all the tithes into the storehouse, that there may be meat in mine house, and prove me now herewith, saith the Lord of hosts, if I will not open you the windows of heaven, and pour you out a blessing, that there shall not be room enough to receive it.

Curses bring slavery and struggle. When man failed God and violated the divine institution in the Garden of Eden to eat the forbidden fruit, God came down and place a curse on the land, that out of great labour and toil shall man eat the fruit of the ground. And that the earth will bring thorns against the harvest. The productive ability and capacity of the earth was reduced by this curse. Man was only to eat through the sweat of his labour. Life hardened up, struggles began. A curse brings life to the dust. The Lord cursed the serpent and said dust shall thou eat all the day of thy life. (Genesis 3 vs. 14)

God's original design for man was to live in abundance without labour, the garden of Eden was planted by the Lord for man, violation of divine instruction drove man out of his dominion into the field of labour and struggle.

Gen 3:17-19

And unto Adam he said, Because thou hast hearkened unto the voice of thy wife, and hast eaten of the tree, of which I commanded thee, saying, Thou shalt not eat of it: cursed is the ground for thy sake; in sorrow shalt thou eat of it all the days of thy life; Thorns also and thistles shall it bring forth to thee; and thou shalt eat the herb of the field; In the sweat of thy face shalt thou eat bread, till thou return unto the ground; for out of it wast thou taken: for dust thou art, and unto dust shalt thou return.

This is the origin of it all man lost his eminent domain to sin of disobedience and became slave and a labourer in his own territory. A curse from the Lord reduced man to dust, a spirit of reproach and desolation, frustration and poverty set in. sweat of face is the key to his bread. But thank God Jesus is the bread of life. He came to break the curse on our bread when he became the bread of life. He brought new life, fruit of abundance and blessing.

Curse destroys freedom and promotes slavery.

Josh 9:23

Now therefore ye are cursed, and there shall none of you be freed from being bondmen, and hewers of wood and drawers of water for the house of my God.

A curse can break your foundation of greatness and reduce you to a mere slave and bondmen, engaging only in the menial, laborious jobs, hewer of wood and drawer of water. Only housemaids perform these in the house. Our people were seen to be bonded in servitude until knowledge of liberty in covenant breaking came with the light and power of total emancipation in the blood of Jesus; we are now free, hallelujah. The strongholds of that covenant are broken in Jesus name.

Josh 7:11-12

Israel hath sinned, and they have also transgressed my covenant which I commanded them: for they have even taken of the accursed thing, and have also stolen, and dissembled also, and they have put it even among their own stuff. Therefore the children of Israel could not stand before their enemies, but turned their backs before their enemies, because they were accursed: neither will I be with you any more, except ye destroy the accursed from among you.

Because of the accursed thing which was brought into the camp of Israel by Achan, God's presence was withdrawn from Israel, they could no longer be able to fight victoriously. They lost every battle and lost lives as well. When we are working under the dominant of a curse, whether directly or indirectly involve, we become defeated and turn our backs on the enemies. The good news is that when the accursed thing is destroyed, the victory returns.

BARRENNESS IS A CURSE

When Abraham and his wife, Sarah settled in the land of Gerar in Genesis 20 and verse two, the Bible says the king of Gerar, Abimelech took Sarah, Abraham's wife and God intervened immediately to stop him from sinning with the wife of the patriarch, so the Lord quickly warned him in the dream and said you are dead man, if you don't restore immediately his wife. While the king was hasty to do this, the Lord had quickly shut the wombs of all the household of Abimelech.

> *Gen 20:17-18*
>
> *So Abraham prayed unto God: and God healed Abimelech, and his wife, and his maidservants; and they bare children. For the Lord had fast closed up all the wombs of the house of Abimelech, because of Sarah Abraham's wife.*

A curse could be inflicted upon innocent people by one wicked act that brings a curse upon the land. Abimelech did it, his wife, maid servants and all wombs in his domain were shut by the Lord in consequent of his lustful act on the wife of Abraham. Most barrenness is a spell of the forbearers on the descendants. Abraham prayed for the king and all his household and the Lord healed them and opened their wombs again. I stand in my prophetic and apostolic office to pray that every curse over your life and family that brings barrenness martially or materially is broken today in Jesus name. You will start to bear fruits forth with in Jesus name. Amen.

UNTIMELY DEATH IS A CURSE

Most of the tragic and untimely deaths in our society are caused by cursed foundation laid by someone, some times.

Josh 6:26

And Joshua adjured them at that time, saying, Cursed be the man before the Lord, that riseth up and buildeth this city Jericho: he shall lay the foundation thereof in his firstborn, and in his youngest son shall he set up the gates of it.

After Jericho was brought down by the power of the Lord, Joshua placed a curse on the city against a reconstruction, that such attempts will be tragic bloodshed. The curse stands because God was with Joshua. Don't joke over a curse pronounced by an anointed man of God, or a Satanic priest if you don't refute immediately in the case of Satanic priest, it holds. Reverse immediately or tell it to an anointed man of God to counter it and send it back. In the case of this scripture, many thousands of years came and pass, people lost memory to it but the curse was still effective watching over for the victim.

EFFECTIVE ON THE VICTIM

1 Kings 16:34

In his days did Hiel the Bethelite build Jericho: he laid the foundation thereof in Abiram his firstborn, and set up the gates thereof in his youngest son Segub, according to the word of the Lord, which he spake by Joshua the son of Nun.

This is a victim of this curse. He lost his first son Abraham and his last son Segub according to the statement of the curse placed by Joshua the man of God. People are still suffering from unknown curses placed on them by ancestors, priests, parents and superiors, and the scope of affliction is determined by the statement of such curses. Hiel's rebuilding effort evoked the foundational curse and landed him in a great tragedy.

Some struggles that result in tragic futility is as a result of trying to build upon cursed foundation. Pray and take counseling surveys. Enquire from the Lord over the strange experience of your life. Don't watch it destroy your life. Ask God for a way out. This particular curse whose foundation was tragic life destruction was reversed by Elisha when the double anointing of Elijah was upon him and the people of the city notice it and consulted with him over the situation of the Land. 2 Kings 2 vs. 19-22.

Hear this prophetic word from the Lord, whatever or whoever placed a curse of death upon your life or family, it is reversed in Jesus name. You shall not die young. The number of your days on earth will be fulfilled. Jesus took our curse on the tree of Calvary that the blessing of Abraham might come unto us. Receive yours right now in Jesus name.

The Bible says a lawful captive shall be delivered. Whatever you have done on the day of ignorant and it is hunting after you today are terminated at the cross of Calvary. You have no case to answer for Jesus said it is finished. I strangle every demonic claim over your life and family. I curse the root to be uprooted in Jesus name. As Jesus cursed the fig tree and it withered from the root so the root of your problem, sickness, barrenness and demonic attacks are withered from the foundations, those charms and evil spell upon your life is destroyed. Every accusing demon is cast out in Jesus name. The chains and the cage of bondage that traps you and hold you sway from your destiny are melted by the power of the Holy Spirit. I declare all demonic monitoring agents to suffocate and die in the ocean of God's judgment in Jesus name. The crystal mirror and the monitoring window in the witchcraft coven are broken and scattered in Jesus name. I summon every force, human spirit and territorial strongholds before the council of divinity for sentencing and extermination. I poison their realm with the blood of Jesus and cause them to drink death in the water of affliction. I fence their territory with the blood of Jesus and lock them in to starve to spiritual death. I announce in the spirit the burial date of everyone that works against your fortune in Jesus name.

Now I take you to the ocean of the blood of Jesus and bath you of all filth and uncleanness and declare you sanctified for the masters use in Jesus name. Your days of fulfillment are announced by the angel of the Lord. The value of your life is restored through the death of Jesus. We mean more to God that he lost his life to get ours. We are back to the kingdom. This is an enforcement of God's power for total deliverance in my case. Shout out, I am free. Amen.

CHAPTER FIVE

SATANIC COVENANTS AND DEMONIC VOWS

2 Kings 17:9-12

And the children of Israel did secretly those things that were not right against the Lord their God, and they built them high places in all their cities, from the tower of the watchmen to the fenced city. And they set them up images and groves in every high hill, and under every green tree: And there they burnt incense in all the high places, as did the heathen whom the Lord carried away before them; and wrought wicked things to provoke the Lord to anger: For they served idols, whereof the Lord had said unto them, Ye shall not do this thing.

16-18

And they left all the commandments of the Lord their God, and made them molten images, even two calves, and made a grove, and worshipped all the host of heaven, and served Baal. And they caused their sons and their daughters to pass through the fire, and used divination and enchantments, and sold themselves to do evil in the sight of the Lord, to provoke him to anger.

Therefore the Lord was very angry with Israel, and removed them out of his sight: there was none left but the tribe of Judah only.

Satanic covenant or vow sells a people, nation to great oppression, slavery and disaster. It takes away the presence of God and puts them into perpetual bondage with Satan.

Any form of worship or sacrifice made unto Satan, enslaves and sells one outright from generation to generation to the spirit that such idol sacrifice was made unto. It hold grips to the descendants except broken. Israel, a chosen nation sold themselves to the worship of Baal and the host of heaven, celestial beings, sacrificed their sons and daughters unto them, this is abomination in the sight of God. They consequently lost their dignity before other nations, defeated in wars; famine was brought upon them till they could not stand the judgment of the Lord.

Solomon never knew that his marriages with the strange women were connecting him in a covenant with the gods and spirits of such lands. This is another development marked the genesis of Israel's involvement in idolatry and demonic worship. Solomon built shrines and high-laces for these familiar spirits, corrupting and polluting the holy nation of Israel. God was wrath with great anger.

1 Kings 11:5,7–8

For Solomon went after Ashtoreth the goddess of the Zidonians, and after Milcom the abomination of the Ammonites.

Then did Solomon build an high place for Chemosh, the abomination of Moab, in the hill that is before Jerusalem, and for Molech, the abomination of the children of Ammon. And likewise did he for all his strange wives, which burnt incense and sacrificed unto their gods.

Solomon covenanted with his strong wives who were Satan's representatives and demonic agents that he was going to serve their gods with them in Israel which he did and that covenant became a thorn in the flesh of the entire nations of Israel. Israel was sold to the service of Baal and other demonic gods through the covenant of marriage made by their king. 100 years later Israel was completely enslaved to the worships of strange spirits and forsook God totally in their lives and activities. Very sad Kings that came were taken after this act in leading Israel to more sins of idolatry. Ahaziah king of Israel was also leading the whole nation to enquire from Baalzebub the gods of Ekron, the prince of the air. 2 Kings 1 vs. 1, 2. The unfortunate thing is that the subsequent generation of Israel was under afflictions, deprivations, wars, famines, confusion and death because of such demonic covenants made by their rulers, Kings and fathers.

Reading from the incidences recorded in the book of first and second Kings, it is clear that the Egyptians and Assyrians regained dominion over the Israelites because they had spiritually submitted to the service of their gods through marriages and satanic consultations by their Kings.

They sold themselves spiritually to these gods and erected shrines and altars as tokens of the covenants and marry their agents. The nations of Israel were in total frustrations and disintegration. Calamities were results of these strange interactions with satanic activities.

WHAT IS A SATANIC COVENANT?

A Satanic covenant is an agreement in which one enters with Satan or demons which have a legal building. It is a mutual agreement with

Satan which affects ones course of life. Like any other covenant, satanic covenant involves a term, a token and a target. These are the properties of an effective satanic covenant. Satanic covenants a time involve satanic agents as witness or a mediator.

SATANIC COVENANT TERM

This refers specific statement of agreement that is uttered to establish the covenant with Satan or demons. It is the term of satanic covenant that determines the scope of activity. That is, what and who the covenant affects or is extended to. It also determines the duration in which it will be affective.

SATANIC COVENANT TARGET

This speaks of the primary objective. That is what is expected to accomplish through its initiations. It is the target that determines the effects and the repercussion of such covenants.

Perhaps, Solomon did not know that covenanting to serve the gods of the strange wives would mean coming under total dominion and affliction by the rulers of the lands from where he married those strange wives and their demonic gods. He never knew that it could cost him and the children the selling out of throne of Israel to demon spirits. Yet these were the target of these strange women when they came into marriage covenant in the land with Solomon.

SATANIC COVENANT TOKEN

This refers to substance, symbols, signs, or medium which serves as a guarantee, memorial, evidence, or seal for the consent of that covenant. This satanic covenant token varies, depending on the satanic covenant involved. It can be living wandering animal, blood of animal or human blood. Of parts, living wandering human (mad), shrines, trees as altars, constituted or devoted feast or rituals, body marks, body cuts, rings, amulets, mirrors, pictures, money saliva or and many other things. These are some of the thing people present to Satan or his demons or his agents as a token for the seal of such demonic covenant to be effective. Since covenant tokens are always contributed by two parties involved, Satan himself also make his provision for any such covenant to win ones interest to initiate. Some of Satan's provisions include, supernatural abilities, e.g. fortune telling, powers, dreams and interpretations, extraordinary knowledge, extraordinary strength, fame, wealth, covenant names, dress, become your spirit husband or wife, singing abilities, dancing skills, jewelry and so on. The act of witchcraft is a complete sell out into satanic covenant of wickedness and destructions. We will deal with this separately in a different chapter.

Manasseh was twelve years old when he began to reign and he reigned fifty-and five years in Jerusalem. And his mother's name was Hephzibah. And he did that which was evil in the sight of the lord, after the abominations of the heathens, whom the Lord cast out before the children of Israel. For he built up again the high places which Hezekiah had destroyed and reared up altars for Baal, and made a grove as did Ahab the King of Israel, and worshipped all the host of heaven and served them. And build altars in the house of the Lord and he build altars for the host of heaven in the two courts of the house of the Lord. And he made his sons to pass through fire (initiation and human sacrifice) and observed times and used enchantments and dealt with familiar spirits and wizards, Manasseh seduced them to do more than did the nations whom the Lord destroyed.

Manasseh king of Judah hath done this abominations and had done wickedly above all that the Amorite did which were before him and had made Judah also to sin in his idols 2 Kings 21 vs. 1-11.

CLASSIFICATION OF SATANIC COVENANTS

Satanic covenants may be classified into two major broad divisions. These are direct and indirect satanic covenants.

(a) DIRECT SATANIC COVENANT

Isa 52:2-3

hake thyself from the dust; arise, and sit down, O Jerusalem: loose thyself from the bands of thy neck, O captive daughter of Zion. For thus saith the Lord, Ye have sold yourselves for nought; and ye shall be redeemed without money.

Ex 32:21-24

And Moses said unto Aaron, What did this people unto thee, that thou hast brought so great a sin upon them? And Aaron said, Let not the anger of my lord wax hot: thou knowest the people, that they are set on mischief. For they said unto me, Make us gods, which shall go before us: for as for this Moses, the man that brought us up out of the land of Egypt, we wot not what is become of him. And I said unto them, Whosoever hath any gold, let them break it off. So they gave it me: then I cast it into the fire, and there came out this calf.

A direct covenant is the one in which one is personally involved in the defining of the term and consented to the making of the covenant. The two scriptures quoted simultaneously shows how one or a nation could enter into the direct covenant with Satan without understanding the damned consequence. When Jesus was betrayed and falsely accused before Pilate and was innocently condemned, the Jews owned up the quilt and said.

Matt 27:25

Then answered all the people, and said, His blood be on us, and on our children.

They establish the sentence and judgment upon themselves and their children. They were ready to bear the consequence and pass on to the succeeding generation to suffer.

Jer 2:34

Also in thy skirts is found the blood of the souls of the poor innocents: I have not found it by secret search, but upon all these.

This scripture in 2 Samuel 1 vs. 14-16 *(And David said unto him, How wast thou not afraid to stretch forth thine hand to destroy the Lord's anointed? And David called one of the young men, and said, Go near, and fall upon him. And he smote him that he died. And David said unto him, Thy blood be upon thy head; for thy mouth hath testified against thee, saying, I have slain the Lord's anointed),* is also confirming personal involvement in acts that initiate into a destructive covenants. It shows how individuals consciously or unconsciously get involve in the covenant by defining the term, providing the token and accepting the token from Satan or any other source for the sealing of the covenant. Such individual may not be aware of what Satan is targeting to accomplish through such covenants. It is always soul trap and destiny destruction.

For instance, Solomon personally went to marry his strange wives and covenanted with them in the service of their gods. This was a direct satanic covenant which he signed against himself. People get hooked in a direct satanic covenants when they go for initiations into mystic cults, occults, such as ekpo, ekpe and other masquerading cults, ndem, witchcraft, magic, fortune telling, sorcery, mbiam and so on, through certain satanic agents and organizations. In such situations, the individuals sold themselves to Satan and his dominion. Many other people in search for protection, victory in wars or other cases, children, business fortune, popularity, spiritual powers, political might and success, money riches and other spiritual aspirations got themselves involved in direct satanic covenants and sol out completely to Satan's dominion.

This direct covenant in the course of time becomes indirect covenant to the succeeding generation or descendants based upon the definition of the term to widen its cover to the unborn by the link of ancestry.

(b) INDIRECT SATANIC COVENANTS

An indirect satanic covenant refers to the one in which an individual, family or community is bound into it by someone else through the expansion of the scope of the terms. The individual, family or community is not directly involved in the definition. Indirect satanic covenants can hold against someone in many ways. One of such is a situation whereby a father or mother enters into a covenant with Satan, and in defining the terms, he or she expanded the scope to cover his or her descendants. *(Mathew 27 vs. 25)*.

For instance, the scope of the covenant can de expanded where a father or a mother uses the words such as "me and my family or household", 'I and all my children" or as long as we shall live or every first son or daughter that shall be born to me, and all mother people after me in their generations etc. satanic covenants established with such utterances are perpetual. All generations of the people are bound under such covenant. *(Genesis 41 vs. 43, 44, Exodus 20 vs. 5, Isaiah 434 vs. 27, Joshua 6 vs. 26 fulfilled in 1 Kings 16 vs. 34)*.

In *Luke 11 vs. 50,51* God required the blood of the prophets slain from this generation. And they caused their sons and daughters to pass through fire, *2 Kings 17 vs. 17.*

2 Kings 21:4-5

And he built altars in the house of the Lord, of which the Lord said, In Jerusalem will I put my name. And he built altars for all the host of heaven in the two courts of the house of the Lord.

These were cases where parents got their children initiated into satanic covenants from tender age. Most people who had parents and ancestors that served and worshipped Satan through different diabolical ways are affected by certain covenants that such parents made with Satan. 2 Kings 9 vs. 7-10, 1 Kings 22 vs. 51-53. Most of the troubles and afflictions that some people or family pass through are direct results of such satanic covenants. Especially in the situations where such spirits are no longer worshipped, appeased and sacrificed to seasonally as the parents of such individuals, families or community covenanted.

Another way in which indirect satanic covenant holds is in a situation where the founding fathers and rulers of a community established a satanic covenant concerning the land, that is, the rulers selling the land and its inhabitants to Satan in a covenant.

Most calamities, confusions, frustrations, oppressions, defeat, death and barrenness that plague the citizens and inhabitants of such lands and community are results of such term of satanic covenants made. Certain peculiar hindrances, hardness, oppositions to the gospel that is observed in certain people, land and communities are resultant of satanic covenants in which the founding fathers and ancestors of such communities established with the spirits in the land thereby selling the land and its inhabitants to Satan 2 Kings 21 vs. 1-16.

The inhabitants may not be aware of such covenants in the land against them. They only suffer the consequence. Many people dedicate their children through several initiations to water spirits even before they are born. Such children grow up in such satanic bondage that their lives function in the negative. In the course of life, Satan may cease their fortune, health, wealth, business, children, careers, family and eventually lost their lives at Satan's convenience except divine interventions. Such people live and struggle under the yoke and spell of Satan till they die.

Whenever an individual define the term of a satanic covenant such that the scope of the covenant touches other people, such will be indirectly affected unknown.

Most people who are bound under this covenant were not directly involved, but the blood or family ties bring them in on the definition of the terms.

CHAPTER SIX

TYPES OF SATANIC COVENANTS

(A) SATANIC COVENANT OF DEATH

This speaks of the covenant or agreement with Satan after fulfilling the demands of initiation which resulted in indiscriminate and untimely death. Here a peculiar demon spirit is assigned to ensure the execution of the covenant term. This demon is referred to as "the spirit of death". When such holds against a family or community, it experiences untimely, mysterious and tragic deaths.

The wife of Jacob, Rachel died in the process of delivering one of her sons Benjamin because unknown to the husband the covenant of death was invited into the family against a victim of the stolen gods of Laban.

> *Gen 31:32*
>
> *With whomsoever thou findest thy gods, let him not live: before our brethren discern thou what is thine with me, and take it to thee. For Jacob knew not that Rachel had stolen them.*

Jacob made this pronouncement before Laban the father of Rachel, not aware that his wife Rachel had stolen the gods. Therefore the spirit of death by this pronouncement hunted after her and got her during child labour.

Gen 35:16

And they journeyed from Bethel; and there was but a little way to come to Ephrath: and Rachel travailed, and she had hard labour.

18-19

And it came to pass, as her soul was in departing, (for she died) that she called his name Ben-oni: but his father called him Benjamin.

19 And Rachel died, and was buried in the way to Ephrath, which is Bethlehem.

This is a monitoring spirit watching over the statement of covenant to ensure the fulfillment. This spirit confronted God over the life of Moses as God was about to take him alive and accused God for violation of law of dead for dead. Today by the name of Jesus and by the authority in the blood of Jesus, the final price for our deliverance, the covenant with death is going top be broken. Ruth 1 vs. 1-5, Psalm 89 vs. 11, Psalm 102 vs. 20.

Isa 28:18

And your covenant with death shall be disannulled, and your agreement with hell shall not stand; when the overflowing scourge shall pass through, then ye shall be trodden down by it.

This is a type of satanic covenant which results in total desolation and death. The demon monitored spirit works to actualize the term which is death, untimely and tragic death. Such covenant stands against the progress of family involved; until the redemptive power of the blood of Jesus is invited as an atonement price for the damnable consequence, only there and then can such deadly covenant be broken and soul bound life set free. The blood paid the price and erases such demonic and deadly covenant away, proclaim freedom to the captive.

Col 2:14-15

Blotting out the handwriting of ordinances that was against us, which was contrary to us, and took it out of the way, nailing it to his cross; And having spoiled principalities and powers, he made a shew of them openly, triumphing over them in it.

This is where the strength of covenant breaking and its effective results is drawn from. The power of the cross blots away every hand writing from any demonic world working against our destiny. The death of Jesus on the cross destroyed it and cleans it up, spoil all their evil terms and bring victory to the victim. The blood of Jesus had power to annul every covenant of death entered ignorantly with Satan. Just confess Jesus as your Lord and Saviour, accept the finish work at Calvary in faith, stand on the full promises of salvation, deliverance and healing, plead the blood over your soul and souls of all the members of the family. Claim a new covenant of life in Jesus. Rehearse aloud with authority the change of covenant foundation and terms as in the book of Hebrews 8 vs. 13.

In that he saith, A new covenant, he hath made the first old. Now that which decayeth and waxeth old is ready to vanish away.

Stand on this command such satanic covenant by the blood of Jesus to decay and vanish away. Then wash yourself and family with the blood of Jesus and be clean.

John 15 vs. 3.

Now ye are clean through the word which I have spoken unto you.

Take a cleansing prayer and fasting for three days in the word of God. Confess your soul salvation and a change of covenant kingdom and power.

Who hath delivered us from the power of darkness, and has translated us into the kingdom of his dear son. In whom we have redemption through his blood, even the forgiveness of sins. (Colossians 1 vs. 13, 14)

(B) SATANIC COVENANT WITH HELL

Satanic covenants are diverse, based on the target of the covenant. Satan who swore he would not stay alone in hell is trapping souls of men bound them in eternal covenant for hell through diverse demonic initiations and occult and witchcraft practices.

Jesus is the only solution to such satanic involvements. Salvation is only in his name. Covenant with hell can be broken in his name and blood.

Isa 28:18

And your covenant with death shall be disannulled, and your agreement with hell shall not stand; when the overflowing scourge shall pass through, then ye shall be trodden down by it.

Covenant; we say in an agreement which have a legal binding. So when we bind ourselves into such covenants, we have entered into a covenant agreement with hell, to be doomed forever. The Bible says what shall we give for the exchange of our souls.

He is the place to eternal punishment for Satan and his followers. So if in any way, one enters into an agreement with Satan, this binds ones soul with him into hell, a place of eternal torment, and unquenchable fire or God's righteous Judgment on Satan and his agents.

Rev 20:12-15

And I saw the dead, small and great, stand before God; and the books were opened: and another book was opened, which is the book of life: and the dead were judged out of those things which were written in the books, according to their works. And the sea gave up the dead which were in it; and death and hell delivered up the dead which were in them: and they were judged every man according to their works. And death and hell were cast into the lake of fire. This is the second death. And whosoever was not found written in the book of life was cast into the lake of fire.

Hell is Satan's final place with his followers. May your covenant agreement with Satan for hell be broken today through the death and resurrection power of Jesus Christ. Amen.

(C) **SATANIC COVENANT OF BONDAGE AND SERVITUDE**

> *The children of Israel were bound by this, cord of bondage and servitude for 430 years in the land Egypt. The served the Egyptians under the severe oppression of the task masters. They were enslaved and afflicted by the Egyptian strongholds until the Lord showed up under the leadership of Moses and brought them out. Now therefore yet are cursed, and there shall none of your be freed from being bondmen, and hewers of wood and drawers of water for the house of my god. Joshua 9 vs. 23.*

Every satanic covenant brings a curse of slavery, bondage and servitude. Such as living on menial Jobs, house boy-ship answering, yes sir for life and the likes. Moses served his father in law until the Lord took him out.

> *1 Sam 11:1-2*

> *Then Nahash the Ammonite came up, and encamped against Jabesh-gilead: and all the men of Jabesh said unto Nahash, Make a covenant with us, and we will serve thee. And Nahash the Ammonite answered them, On this condition will I make a covenant with you, that I may thrust out all your right eyes, and lay it for a reproach upon all Israel.*

Nahash, the Ammonites worshipped Molek and Milcom (1 Kings 11 vs. 5, 7). Yet the men of Jabesh-gileed wanted to sell their land and people to Nahash and their gods in servitude. They wanted to covenant for a temporal protection that will plunge the entire land and people into a covenanted servitude.

The children of Israel once told Gideon "rule thou over us both thou and thy sons and son's son also. Gideon wisely told them, I will not rule over you neither shall my son rule over you. The Lord shall rule over you (Judges 8 vs. 22, 23).

This situation with Gideon was because he was not a satanic agent or demonic prince. What do we say to those who make similar covenants with demons and demonic agents? This is a satanic covenant of servitude and bondage.

A satanic covenant of servitude speaks of an agreement which is made with Satan or his agents resulting in people being directly in service to Satan. Most times its covenant is enforced with Satan, when people go to Satan to seek for powers, favour or political fortune or child are bound to be initiated and such a child will grow to be fully initiated into satanic kingdom. Those who seek money through this diabolical means seal their soul into eternal covenant of bondage and servitude to Satan. Their lives and possessions are all influenced by Satan and will destroy them at will without notice or mercy.

(D) **SATANIC COVENANT OF SICKNESS**

Most of the strange diseases and sickness that are current today and defy the medical efforts are demonic inflictions. Incurable sickness, heredity and ancestral occurrences often times are covenant founded. Once this covenant is entered, all health-monitored demons are assigned.

The token from the sick person through any diabolical means is taken to the witchcraft coven, with it; they can monitor the victim and afflict him with strange and incurable disease.

Luke 13:11-13

And, behold, there was a woman which had a spirit of infirmity eighteen years, and was bowed together, and could in no wise lift up herself. And when Jesus saw her, he called her to him, and said unto her, Woman, thou art loosed from thine infirmity. And he laid his hands on her: and immediately she was made straight, and glorified God.

This was a demonic spirit of infirmity. It blows her down; every medical attention given to her did not yield result. Jesus rebuked the spirit and the woman was free. You will be free from all demonic sickness and diseases in Jesus name. There are many cases in the Bible that disease and sickness refuse to yield result on medical effort but Jesus is always the source of such healing miracles.

Matt 9:20-21

And, behold, a woman, which was diseased with an issue of blood twelve years, came behind him, and touched the hem of his garment:

21 For she said within herself, If I may but touch his garment, I shall be whole.

Only the anointing in the name of Jesus destroys such demonic yoke of sickness. In Exodus 15 vs. 29. The Lord said, I am the Lord that heals thee. The power to break demonic yoke of sickness comes from the Lord.

Isa 10:27

And it shall come to pass in that day, that his burden shall be taken away from off thy shoulder, and his yoke from off thy neck, and the yoke shall be destroyed because of the anointing.

Anointing destroys every satanic spell of sickness. Whatever you are carrying about from the kingdom of darkness, defying every medical application, I curse that thing out in the name of Jesus Christ. I command you to be loosed from the chains of bondage and sickness in Jesus name. Plead the blood of Jesus over your health and the health of your entire family, claim healing and deliverance from sickness in Jesus name. Amen.

(E) SATANIC COVENANT OF FRUSTRATION AND FAILURE

This is a satanic covenant holding against individuals which result in a demon monitored frustration and near success syndrome in their endeavours. Here, an evil spirit is assigned to closely monitor the activities of the individual and thwart them. Such life is subject to struggle and hardship. Easy things for others become so difficult for him to overcome. If it holds against a family, nobody make meaning in life in the entire family. God promised to frustrate the token of the liars and to make diviners mad.

By the power of resurrection, the spell of frustration and cobweb of desolation is broken in Jesus name. I declare you free and to succeed in your endeavours in Jesus name. The chains are broken, step out with boldness and make a land slide breakthrough in your life in Jesus name. Peter confessing to Jesus said Master we have toiled all night and caught nothing, nevertheless, at thy word. I declare by the authority of the word of God that every spirit of struggle and toil over your life and family is destroyed in Jesus name. When the son sets you free, you are free indeed. You are free today, go and prosper in your life. Amen.

SATANIC COVENANT OF WAR

This is an agreement made with Satan which results in absence of peace. The Bible says to the wicked there shall be no peace. So the spirit of war, violent and riots and incessant land disputes and bloodshed will be experienced by the citizens of such land. No peace.

Ezek 8:17

Then he said unto me, Hast thou seen this, O son of man? Is it a light thing to the house of Judah that they commit the abominations which they commit here? for they have filled the land with violence, and have returned to provoke me to anger: and, lo, they put the branch to their nose.

This abominable practice evokes wars, violence, riots and all other forms of social vices capable of deterring peace and progress in the land. It causes inter-communal wars, troubles of various magnitudes resulting in blood shed to appease the spirit behind such covenant.

SATANIC COVENANT THROUGH VISIT TO HERBALISTS AND NATIVE DOCTORS

Herbalists and native doctors are those traditional medicine practitioners using herbs and roots concoction to treat some problem natively. To function effectively in this, they mostly have affiliate initiation in the realm of evil spirits for powers and information about roots and herbs and their uses. Demon spirit responsible for this establishes covenant traits with them before such revelation practices associated with ancestral link and those who consult with them either for treatment, enquiry or herbs concoction are initiated through the door ways established in this ritualistic performance. They also work in close association with the witchcraft coven to pass information of trap across. Those who open up their lives unto them, through sometimes, palm reading, fortune telling and or concoction for child bearing and marriage fortune are direct victims of these initiations.

They access your destiny and release a demon monitoring spirit to follow up.

> *2 Kings 1:2-4*
>
> *And Ahaziah fell down through a lattice in his upper chamber that was in Samaria, and was sick: and he sent messengers, and said unto them, Go, inquire of Baal-zebub the god of Ekron whether I shall recover of this disease. But the angel of the Lord said to Elijah the Tishbite, Arise, go up to meet the messengers of the king of Samaria, and say unto them, Is it not because there is not a God in Israel, that ye go to inquire of Baal-zebub the god of Ekron? Now therefore thus saith the Lord, Thou shalt not come down from that bed on which thou art gone up, but shalt surely die. And Elijah departed.*

Here we see that from the ancient times people consult with demon spirits through their agents about their sickness, disease, and other state of their social or private lives, bringing a curse or demonic attacks upon their lives and family or community.

(1 Samuel28 vs. 7-9).

You see this agents operation with familiar spirits and wizards. They work together. To snare and trap the life of the victim who consult with them. It is demonic. Don't try it; it initiates you and your bloodline into Satanism. Call upon God in the day of trouble he will deliver you.

Ps 50:15

And call upon me in the day of trouble: I will deliver thee, and thou shalt glorify me.

God is the only way to salvation and deliverance. Seek him and you will find him. He is the present help in times of need.

PROPHETIC CONFESSION/PRAYER

In the mighty name of Jesus, I take authority in the word of God as the sword of the spirit over every satanic covenant of death, Hell, barrenness, frustration and demonic sickness. I declare their spell over my life and family, directly or indirectly broken, I reject and forsake their terms over my life, I denounce totally their claim over my soul, and I untie my soul from their strongholds in Jesus name. Their cord of affliction over me is broken. I sprinkle the blood of Jesus over my soul in Jesus name Amen.

CHAPTER SEVEN

BREAKING THE CORDS OF WITCHCRAFT

Witchcraft is one of the elemental black arts of ancient which is perpetuated in the act of wickedness, destructions, death and misfortune. It is detestable in the sight of God.

Lev 19:31

Regard not them that have familiar spirits, neither seek after wizards, to be defiled by them: I am the Lord your God.

God is against the spirit of witchcraft. They defile and abuse victims, they are blood sucking, fortune destroyer, and their activities are divergent in nature. They are ultimate practice of wickedness, killing, causing accidents, barrenness and business hard up. It is destructive, fights progress and enemy of light. God cursed them and those who practice this or consult with them for whatever reason contradict divine nature and abuse his soul for eternal damnation. You are dead perpetually. They trap souls for destruction and desolation.

Lev 20:6

And the soul that turneth after such as have familiar spirits, and after wizards, to go a whoring after them, I will even set my face against that soul, and will cut him off from among his people.

God is vehement against them and whoever is associated or consult with them in defiled and God promises to judge such souls to destroy and to cut off from his people. Witchcraft is one of the worst and wicked practices in satanic kingdom. Once initiated, that soul is abomination in the sight of God, God hates and will not spare them.

"Thou shall not suffer a witch to live." Exodus 22 vs. 18

Those who operate with such wicked spirits in them have defiled God's nature in them; they are corrupted in their imaginations. They work against every plan and purpose of God; they hate righteousness, progress and blessing. God will not spare them, their judgment has come already.

Isa 8:19

And when they shall say unto you, Seek unto them that have familiar spirits, and unto wizards that peep, and that mutter: should not a people seek unto their God? for the living to the dead?

The activities of witchcraft and familiar spirits are spelt out here. Their works involve peeping. To peep means to trying to have access through a hole or door way into the future or secret plans of someone in order to block or frustrate them. They monitor using spell and crystal witchcraft ball on the victim to strike the soul in their coven for sudden death or misfortune. They peep through witchcraft mirror into the womb of a pregnant woman either to eat out the embryo or to cause miscarriage. They peep into successful marriage or business and destroy them by casting spell of anger, bitterness and failures. The word mutter is defining one of their ways of operations. To strike, when they peep through the windows of your destiny to see the future, they strike with hazards, dead or sorrows. They strike through a peaceful and loving marriage and ruin sets in. They are the spirits behind most family misfortunes, dead, accidents, infant morality, barrenness, academic failures, miscarriages, spirit husbands or spirit wives, eating in dreams, spirit children, masquerades pursuing and diversity of violence, rebellion and rejection, frustration, paganism, poverty, stubbornness and resistance to the gospel of Jesus Christ to bring light and salvation of souls.

1 Sam 15:23

For rebellion is as the sin of witchcraft, and stubbornness is as iniquity and idolatry. Because thou hast rejected the word of the Lord, he hath also rejected thee from being king.

It releases demons of disobedience and stubbornness, rejection to the word of God. It works with ancestral spirit of the family to establish and initiate their aims. The bible talks about the spirit that now move in the children of disobedience. It is the spirit of witchcraft aiming at destroying that soul to bring eternal consequence on the victim, please pray always and read the word of God.

NECROMANCY

This is another form of witchcraft practice which deals with the invocation of the spirit of the dead. Often, the spirit of an occult grandmaster is invoked to operate or the spirit of a certain person in the family that had certain relevance in the activity of the living is invoked either for inquiry or for a destructive assignments. This act of necromancy is always performed by a witch or a wizard. A wizard is a male agent in the witchcraft operations.

1 Sam 28:7

Then said Saul unto his servants, Seek me a woman that hath a familiar spirit, that I may go to her, and inquire of her. And his servants said to him, Behold, there is a woman that hath a familiar spirit at Endor.

This is a witchcraft activity dealing with the spirit of dead. They call it familiar spirit, have details about your family and are familiar with everything that is going on in your life. Monitoring through the windows of your soul they access through family tokens, like umbilical cord of a particular person buried under a tree in the family specific place or other tokens, like nail cut, incision, and night body scratch, money collected to witch coven or satanic altar, satanic feasting, drinking concoction devoted to a spirit. All these are doorways which open your life windows to these demon spirits of witchcrafts.

Whenever you consult with the agents of these spirits you re bringing a curse of God upon your life and also completely sold out to demonic worlds.

1 Sam 28:11

Then said the woman, Whom shall I bring up unto thee? And he said, Bring me up Samuel.

This is satanic; invoking the spirit of dead to inquire or to talk with, instantly your soul is initiated into witchcraft with the spirit of dead. The Bible says we should seek after the living God. And enquire from him in his temple. Hannah enquired of him in the temple; the Lord hearkened unto her and blessed her. David inquired of the lord and the Lord answered him and gave him direction which led to his victory and recovery. Secret things belong to the Lord.

> *Deut 18:10-14*
>
> *There shall not be found among you any one that maketh his son or his daughter to pass through the fire, or that useth divination, or an observer of times, or an enchanter, or a witch, Or a charmer, or a consulter with familiar spirits, or a wizard, or a necromancer. For all that do these things are an abomination unto the Lord: and because of these abominations the Lord thy God doth drive them out from before thee. Thou shalt be perfect with the Lord thy God.*

CORDS

This is witchcraft thread with which they tie, link one to their traps and coven. It is soul ties that communicate and link up the victim and puts him on hold until their final verdict is taken on him.

> *Ps 129:4*
>
> *The Lord is righteous: he hath cut asunder the cords of the wicked.*

Every demonic cord that connects you and your family to witchcraft coven, I declare in the name of Jesus, the righteous Lord to be broken and your soul set free. I declare the same cord of the wicked to hold on the wicked according to the word of God.

Prov 5:22

His own iniquities shall take the wicked himself, and he shall be holden with the cords of his sins.

Isa 5:18

Woe unto them that draw iniquity with cords of vanity, and sin as it were with a cart rope:

I stand on the foundation of the blood of Jesus to cause every cord of affliction, desolation and barrenness broken in Jesus name. Whenever they rope you, with the sword of the spirit the rope is cut, the captive soul is delivered. Jump out of their coven for your soul is free, that cord that holds you for death is broken, and your soul is escaped. **Psalm 124:7.** Thank God for untying your soul from the cords of witchcraft operations.

BREAKING THE SPELL AND WITCHCRAFT MONITORING WINDOWS

Just as we saw in Isaiah 8:19, the monitoring window is the peeping pinhole into the veins of ones destiny. It is a hunting spirit from the witch coven. It is the spirit of Jezebel, the queen of witchcraft. It impersonates disguises to lay in wait for the victim. This spirit dominates and chairs every activity in the central witchcraft coven where universal decision for principal destruction is taken. It can trap a whole nation and bring to desolation, destroy kings and champions, using activities designed in the coven as a trap e.g. women fashion for a trap of a targeted person, or business designed to trap the greedy and lustful victims. It controls government and bewitch leaders. Jezebel was the one who determined the decision of King Ahab through her spirit of witchcraft.

2 Kings 9:7

And thou shalt smite the house of Ahab thy master, that I may avenge the blood of my servants the prophets, and the blood of all the servants of the Lord, at the hand of Jezebel.

22

And it came to pass, when Joram saw Jehu, that he said, Is it peace, Jehu? And he answered, What peace, so long as the whoredoms of thy mother Jezebel and her witchcrafts are so many?

We need anointing to deal with this wicked spirit of witchcraft which have trapped and snared many lives through their subtle and wicked activities. Killer of talents and God's generals in all time, I curse it in the name of Jesus.

2 Kings 9:30

And when Jehu was come to Jezreel, Jezebel heard of it; and she painted her face, and tired her head, and looked out at a window.

They go about collecting information, about people, family, who is to marry, which business to attack, which marriage to scatter or who are we trapping in tragic death. They come in disguising nature to operate. She painted her face; this is to look different and deceptive, in order to accomplish the intentions. She looked out in a window, she saw Jehu ever before Jehu came near; they watch the future, trap the innocence. Every witchcraft window with which they view your life plans, I destroy them with the hailstone of God in Jesus name. I command thunder to level the structure to the foundation in the mighty name of Jesus. Every impersonating spirit casting spell upon your life, marriage, wearing the face of the wide or husband to seduce one into sexual insanity in dream, I break the cord of their operations in Jesus name. That demon manipulated in the witchcraft coven to marry you, feed you in dreams, produce children by you in dreams engaging you in slavery labour and spell of bad lucks, I curse them in the blood of Jesus. Their token is frustrated and avoided, the cord is broken, the term of such covenant dismantled, and I call your soul in the name of Jesus to come out of their nets.

2 Kings 11:1-3

And when Athaliah the mother of Ahaziah saw that her son was dead, she arose and destroyed all the seed royal. But Jehosheba, the daughter of king Joram, sister of Ahaziah, took Joash the son of Ahaziah and stole him from among the king's sons which were slain; and they hid him, even him and his nurse, in the bedchamber from Athaliah, so that he was not slain. And he was with her hid in the house of the Lord six years. And Athaliah did reign over the land.

Witchcraft spirit is destiny destroyer. They have mercy on the children or grand children they kill all. Athaliah a witch mother of Ahaziah took over from his son after killing him. She went ahead to kill all the potential and possible successors of the throne, the royal seed. The enemy is always after the royal seed, God's given potential. But Joash was hid in the bedchamber in the house of God. God will hide you and your family from their wicked acts until God's purpose for your life is actualized.

CALLING THE SOUL OF MEN FROM THE WITCHCRAFT COVEN

Even as the Lord Jesus called the soul of Lazarus who was dead already for four days out of the grave and commanded that the grave clothes be loosed from him, I take authority in the name and the blood of Jesus to call the souls of men out of the witchcraft coven. SAY THIS AFTER ME: Oh my soul, by the blood of Jesus the final price for my freedom I stand to call you out of every trap and spell of witchcraft, whether bound in the water kingdom, or in the terrestrial realm or in the market square or in the central junction, I call you in the voice of the Lord to come out, every cord be broken, every cord be broken, every cobweb of frustration be broken, every cage melt like candle wax, whatever token they use to get my soul into grave and coven of bad luck and desolation. As Peter came out of the prison the same night, tonight, my soul and everything that belongs to me, I invoke all out of the realm of witchcraft in Jesus name. I pack all my belongings from the coven of witchcrafts and follows the commanding march out parade of the angel of the Lord, I see myself appearing in God's realm of power and liberty. I am being transported from the kingdom of darkness into the kingdom of God through the blood of Jesus. I am free.

Col 1:13

Who hath delivered us from the power of darkness, and hath translated us into the kingdom of his dear Son:

BREAKING THE SPELL OF LIMITATION.

It is a known fact that all contentions and manipulations in the kingdom of darkness is to stifle and oppress the potential manifestation of the destiny of people. One of such ways is through casting of evil spells on such people. This may be evident in some noticeable setbacks, frustration and life's progress completely retarded. At this point, advancement in every area of endeavor is adversely halted. The result of this leaves one in a great state of depression with the consequence of leaving you far behind equals. In severe cases, the victim is being reduced to a mere living statue with no real life values.

What is a spell?

This is a monitoring window in the realm of darkness whereby innocent lives are being subjected to strange spiritual resistance, setback, hard luck, mishap, failures and complete misfortune in all efforts, spiritually, emotionally and socioeconomically. The victim or victims become a target and monitored through evil spirits assigned to carry out the operations in order to trap, block or cast a cloak of grievous consequences whereby paralyzing every adventure in such a life. In most cases, it forestalls the chances of deliverance whose endpoint is death.

How does one become a victim?

Certain ignorant activities one gets involved in opens some doorway unconsciously to such infiltrations. Such acts create legal windows for divers' spirits with assigned functions to infiltrate the soul of their victims. These activities are various in nature to include: evil association with satanic agents, occultist initiations, blood covenants with evil incantations, taking of blood oath, deceitfully, invocation or consulting with the spirit of the dead (necromancy), involving vicious arts, charms making or wearing, worshipping evil spirits, witchcraft, immoral relationship with evil partners, drink and concoction covenants, ancestral ties, violation of ancestral oath, breaching the trust of allegiance.

All these and many more have the tendency to cast deadly spells of limitations on victims until broken.

Solution:

If any man be in Christ, he is a new creature, old things have passed away. Jesus is the ultimate solution to the dying world. Accepting Jesus as your Lord and savior with an open confession of the involvement and willingly denouncing all evil activities breaks the siege and closes all the known and unknown evil windows. Furthermore, seeking the face of God through prayer, intensive intercession, study of the word of God with the intention to grow in the knowledge of God's principle of kingdom operations. Also, taking counseling sessions with an anointed man of God who is vested with the knowledge of covenant breaking, who will anoint and pray over you with a lead word in evil covenant breaking process and final abstinence from every related act that could lead to further entanglement will proffer God's way of lasting solutions.

CHAPTER EIGHT

EVIDENCES OF SATANIC COVENANTS

This chapter is designed to focus every closely on some signs and proofs of satanic covenant activities in life, family or community. Every satanic covenant, no matter how disguising it might be, will manifest sooner or later noticeable evidence. These evidences are the demonic symptoms which are necessary in demonic symptoms which are necessary in diagnosis and spiritual discernment of demonic afflictions and bondages. These spiritual diagnoses are very useful in the fruitful process of such deliverance. This chapter is one of the underlined prominent chapters that must be well understood.

Evidences of satanic covenants may be classified into two categories: spiritual evidences and visible evidences.

Spiritual evidences are those spiritual manifestations which on most occasions, only the victim is conscious of. The individual is very conscious of such manifestations in the spirit realm of dreams and visions.

Visible evidences speak of those manifestations that are visibly seen and physically noticed. Let us consider some of these evidences specifically.

1. DREAM EXPERIENCES:

Dream world is a realm of revelation. However, it is not every dream that is a revelation; some are result of weaknesses and weariness of the body and much business stress.

> *Eccl 5:3*
>
> *For a dream cometh through the multitude of business; and a fool's voice is known by multitude of words.*
>
> 7
>
> *For in the multitude of dreams and many words there are also divers vanities: but fear thou God.*

This scripture shows that not all dreams of negative feelings are the result of satanic covenant. However, dream experiences are seen to be most outspoken manifestation of satanic covenants because, during sleep, the body and the soul is at rest, the spirit can freely associate with other spirits related to the physical experience of the person. E.g. a woman who dream and see herself making love with unknown person or bearing children shows a demonic contamination of marriage and child bearing, chances of victim.

Different dream reveals different kind of demonic association and satanic complications. In the example case above, the woman will have diverse experiences such as: romance, sexual intercourse with strange or familiar person in dream, giving birth to children in dream, having and keeping matrimonial homes, beautiful dresses in dream, breastfeeding babies or being pregnant in dreams.

A demonic covenant of frustration may be evidenced with such dreams as trading and making gains, receiving money from strange individuals or meeting with witchcraft impersonated animals such as dogs, cats, rats, swine, snakes, monkeys and birds like vulture and other unclean birds.

Other dream evident activities includes having visitations and associations with dead relatives or some one not even very close, cooking and serving a group of people, swimming in streams or river, receiving clothes, shoes, jewelries, cosmetics such as power, perfume and underwear, ring or earrings.

2. LIFE EXPERIENCES:

Individuals live experiences also points to a satanic covenant and bondages. Such experiences like:

- Bad luck in almost every area of endeavour,
- Cobwebs running on your forehead or eyes,
- Showing a demonic blockade and barriers,
- Depression and restlessness
- Constant broken marriage engagement and inability to get marriage partner at all.
- Constant failures in examination or seeing yourself in the former elementary school.

Setbacks on projects that started well, some evidences associated with individual character are: sexual promiscuity, drunkenness, drug addiction, stealing, stubbornness, gluttony and chains of nightmares.

3. SPIRIT VISITATIONS:

This is another definite evidence of satanic association, visitation of demon spirits. It may happen regularly or periodic. Demons transform themselves into many things and try to manifest themselves to their victims in diverse forms. They transform themselves into men to visit

85

women and vice versa to have romance and sexual intercourse. Water spirits visit individuals in the similar way. Demons also visit people in offices and market place based on the covenant altar of such places. Some of these demonic activities capture the interest of the victims because of deceptive manifestation of some traits such as impartation of certain abilities like future telling, dream interpretation, singing, dancing, boxing, wrestling and so on.

Other evidences of spirit visitation include a mysterious disappearance of one's items which may later be seen somewhere, or being used by somebody in a dream or hearing of strange voices calling their names or speaking to them without seeing anybody. At times, strange odours may come from an individual or house with difficulty in discovering the cause, or hearing footsteps behind without seeing anybody.

1. PHYSICAL INFIRMITIES

Some physical infirmities are evidence of some demonic activities of some demonic activities going on in such a life. Such infirmities include mysterious disappearance of a confirmed pregnancy, continuous miscarriages, premature births without any detected defect, periodic sickness, repeated untimely death in the family, some strange epidemic outbreak.

In all these, when one comes under the power of the blood of Jesus for cleansing and forgiveness of sins, repenting over every misdeed and confess Jesus as his Lord and Saviour. Then the power of the Holy Spirit breaks all these yokes and entanglements and sets such life free.

CHAPTER NINE

STEPS TO BREAKING SATANIC COVENANTS AND CURSES

1. YOU MUST BE BORN AGAIN

The first and perhaps, the most important steps to breaking of satanic covenants and curses are for one to be sure of his soul salvation experience. Every unsaved individual is in a covenant of hell with Satan. A sinner is a slave to Satan and cannot break any covenant entanglement with Satan without being born again.

> *1 John 3:8*
>
> *He that committeth sin is of the devil; for the devil sinneth from the beginning. For this purpose the Son of God was manifested, that he might destroy the works of the devil.*

To be of the devil means belonging to the devil and at enmity with God, such person cannot enjoy the liberty and peace of God, except he repents and be saved.

Isa 57:20-21

But the wicked are like the troubled sea, when it cannot rest, whose waters cast up mire and dirt. There is no peace, saith my God, to the wicked.

The sinner is the net of demons and can be used for anything, anytime and anywhere. It is Adam's disobedience to God's word that signed a covenant with hell. For it to be annulled, we must change the Adamic nature through the experience of new birth in Christ Jesus.

When one is born again, he becomes a child of God; Satan lost ownership over his soul.

John 1:12

But as many as received him, to them gave he power to become the sons of God, even to them that believe on his name:

1 Thess 5:23

And the very God of peace sanctify you wholly; and I pray God your whole spirit and soul and body be preserved blameless unto the coming of our Lord Jesus Christ.

Total sanctification, cleanses us from all demonic infiltrations and makes you a vessel unto God for his own use.

Col 1:13-14

Who hath delivered us from the power of darkness, and hath translated us into the kingdom of his dear Son: In whom we have redemption through his blood, even the forgiveness of sins:

Accepting Jesus and the work of redemption accomplished for us on the cross, undertakes our transfer from the kingdom of darkness into the kingdom of God. We are now called sons of God.

Col 1:20-22

And, having made peace through the blood of his cross, by him to reconcile all things unto himself; by him, I say, whether they be things in earth, or things in heaven. And you, that were sometime alienated and enemies in your mind by wicked works, yet now hath he reconciled In the body of his flesh through death, to present you holy and unblameable and unreproveable in his sight:

Jesus had finished the work of our salvation, deliverance and restoration on the cross of his death. When we accept him, we accept all he provides for our salvation, deliverance and liberty. The Bible says *"whomsoever the son sets free, is free indeed"* John. 8:36. I command you to step out for your freedom from bondage of Satan through the blood of Jesus.

2 Cor 6:15-17

And what concord hath Christ with Belial? or what part hath he that believeth with an infidel? And what agreement hath the temple of God with idols? for ye are the temple of the living God; as God hath said, I will dwell in them, and walk in them; and I will be their God, and they shall be my people. Wherefore come out from among them, and be ye separate, saith the Lord, and touch not the unclean thing; and I will receive you,

This is total change of ownership at new birth into the family of God. Old things are now become new.

2 Cor 5:17

Therefore if any man be in Christ, he is a new creature: old things are passed away; behold, all things are become new.

This is the beginning of a life transformation and a change of both spiritual experience and spiritual environment.

2. DISCOVER THE COVENANT

One can only find solution to the problem he has been able to discover. One must be able to clearly discover the type of satanic covenant holding in his life before he gets to break it. When you know the truth, the truth will make you free. To attempt to break a covenant you have not clearly discovered is like boxing the air. Paul, the apostle said; *(1 Corinthians 9 vs. 26)*

Sometimes, you may need to ask questions and collect information from necessary channels such as parents, grandparents; family head and other elders of the community to enable you gather the specimen knowledge of what might be going on. Sometimes, facts finding is indispensable in covenant breaking process. This process of facts finding will enable one to know, how the covenant came about, the term, the token and the purpose it was meant to accomplish.

Jer 33:3

all unto me, and I will answer thee, and shew thee great and mighty things, which thou knowest not.

The best way of facts finding is through deep intercessory prayer with fasting on a topical issue that is relative to the covenant origin and possible way out.

3. REPENTANT AND CONFESSION

Repentance and confession is one of the most important stages in the breaking of satanic covenants.

> *Rom 10:9-10*
>
> *That if thou shalt confess with thy mouth the Lord Jesus, and shalt believe in thine heart that God hath raised him from the dead, thou shalt be saved. For with the heart man believeth unto righteousness; and with the mouth confession is made unto salvation.*
>
> *James 5:16*
>
> *Confess your faults one to another, and pray one for another, that ye may be healed. The effectual fervent prayer of a righteous man availeth much.*
>
> *Neh 1:6*
>
> *Let thine ear now be attentive, and thine eyes open, that thou mayest hear the prayer of thy servant, which I pray before thee now, day and night, for the children of Israel thy servants, and confess the sins of the children of Israel, which we have sinned against thee: both I and my father's house have sinned.*

Prayer that draws the power of God to forgive and deliver or restore is made with confession and repentance. Nehemiah owned up the sins of Israel and asked for total forgivingness from the God of mercy and grace. A broken and a contrite heart God will not despise.

1 Sam 7:3

And Samuel spake unto all the house of Israel, saying, If ye do return unto the Lord with all your hearts, then put away the strange gods and Ashtaroth from among you, and prepare your hearts unto the Lord, and serve him only: and he will deliver you out of the hand of the Philistines.

Ezra 10:10

And Ezra the priest stood up, and said unto them, Ye have transgressed, and have taken strange wives, to increase the trespass of Israel.

The key in all these scriptures is total repentance and confession with a willingness to turn away from it, then the Lord of grace and mercy forgives and brings deliverance and restoration to his people. It works this way always to receive total cleansing and pardon.

Acts 19:18

And many that believed came, and confessed, and shewed their deeds.

Confession exposes it, disgrace it and repentance feels godly sorrow about it, forsakes and denounce it and ask God to forgive it. The Bible says God is faithful and just to forgive our sins.

Isa 55:7

Let the wicked forsake his way, and the unrighteous man his thoughts: and let him return unto the Lord, and he will have mercy upon him; and to our God, for he will abundantly pardon.

4. FAST AND PRAY FOR SPIRITUAL CLEANSING

Waiting upon the Lord in prayer and fasting with serious meditation on the word of God, opens up your spirit to the power and the spirit of God for cleansing and total purging. Fasting energizes and speeds up deliverance process by the spirit of God. It brings the flesh under subjection. There are some levels of demonic activities that can only be broken by prayer and fasting:

Matt 17:19

Then came the disciples to Jesus apart, and said, Why could not we cast him out?

21

Howbeit this kind goeth not out but by prayer and fasting.

Prayer and fasting break the demonic grips on the souls of individual and through the word of God cast them out.

Isa 58:6

Is not this the fast that I have chosen? to loose the bands of wickedness, to undo the heavy burdens, and to let the oppressed go free, and that ye break every yoke?

It is more evident here how effective prayer and fasting destroys the yoke of Satan, looses every band of wickedness and sets the oppressed free. You will be free in Jesus name.

5. BE MINISTERED TO BY AN ANOINTED MAN OF GOD

Gen 20:17

So Abraham prayed unto God: and God healed Abimelech, and his wife, and his maidservants; and they bare children.

How God anointed Jesus of Nazareth with the Holy Ghost and with power: who went about doing good, and hearing all that were oppressed of the devil; for God was with him. **Acts 10:37**

That word, I say, ye know, which was published throughout all Judaea, and began from Galilee, after the baptism which John preached;

This signs shall follow them that believe; in my name shall they cast out devils;... They shall lay hands on the sick, and they shall recover.

Matt 16:17-18

And Jesus answered and said unto him, Blessed art thou, Simon Barjona: for flesh and blood hath not revealed it unto thee, but my Father which is in heaven. And I say also unto thee, That thou art Peter, and upon this rock I will build my church; and the gates of hell shall not prevail against it.

Is any among you afflicted? Let him pray... Is any sick among you? Let him call for the elders of the church; and let them pray over him, anointing him with oil in the name of the Lord; and the prayer of faith shall save the sick, and the Lord shall raise him up; and if he had committed sins, they shall be forgiven him. **James 5 vs. 13-15.**

And the Lord said unto him; Arise, and go into the street which I called straight, and inquire in the house of Judas for one called Saul of Tarsus: for behold, he prayed, and had seen in a vision a man name Ananias coming in, and putting his hand on him, that he might receive his sight. And Ananias went his way, and entered into the house; and putting his hands on him said, Brother Saul, the Lord, even Jesus, that appeared unto thee in the way as thou comest, hasdth sent me that thou mightiest receive thy sight, and be filled with the Holy Ghost. And immediately there fell from his eyes as it had been scales: and he received sight forthwith, and arose, and was baptized. **Acts. 9 vs. 11,12,17,18.**

"And Joshua the son of Nun was full of the spirit of wisdom; for Moses had laid his hands upon him…" Deuteronomy 34 vs. 9.

All these Biblical references at a stretch is to establish the important and prominent functions of being anointed and prayed for by someone called and highly anointed in the area of deliverance. Such ministration takes authority on you over every demonic activity and also brings in the presence of the Holy Ghost to take over such life. Please be prayed for, by some one you trust has a right standing with God and in anointed to deal with yokes and strongholds. When the son sets you free, you shall be free indeed.

6. REVERSE THE COVENANT TERM, DESTROY THE TOKEN AND REJECT THE TARGET

Personal confession, denunciation with the corporate anointing of a minister under whom you submit is very important in breaking satanic covenant. Confess, forsake and exercise authority in the word of God and through the blood of Jesus over every term or token of covenant with which you were roped in destroyed. Bring the word of God as the sword of the spirit and break every satanic cord over your soul, family or community and repent over all evil activity and ask for cleansing. The power to break this covenant is in your commitment to make strong declarations: *Heb 8:13*

> *In that he saith, A new covenant, he hath made the first old. Now that which decayeth and waxeth old is ready to vanish away.*

This scripture shows that things happen as soon as you begin to declare. The satanic covenant tokens are decaying and the terms and targets are ready to vanish away when you announce a change to new covenant with the blood of Jesus. The sacrifice for this to be effective had already been done. Jesus on the cross said it is finished and yielded the ghost. Full price for our deliverance paid. Thank God.

Isa 44:25

> *That frustrateth the tokens of the liars, and maketh diviners mad; that turneth wise men backward, and maketh their knowledge foolish;*

With this scripture, you see God is working with you. Every declaration made at this point is very important because the strength of any covenant is in the power of the spoken word. The Bible says by your words you have ensnared yourself. So through the quickening word of God, you can reverse those negative terms and destroy the token. To frustrate means to render it ineffective and void of function every token, nail cut, saliva, blood, money, private underwear, hair cut, or whatever it is that linked you as a token. I declare them frustrated and destroyed in Jesus name.

1 Sam 7:3-4

> *And Samuel spake unto all the house of Israel, saying, If ye do return unto the Lord with all your hearts, then put away the strange gods and Ashtaroth from among you, and prepare your hearts unto the Lord, and serve him only: and he will deliver you out of the hand of the*

Philistines. Then the children of Israel did put away Baalim and Ashtaroth, and served the Lord only.

2 Chron 31:1

Now when all this was finished, all Israel that were present went out to the cities of Judah, and brake the images in pieces, and cut down the groves, and threw down the high places and the altars out of all Judah and Benjamin, in Ephraim also and Manasseh, until they had utterly destroyed them all. Then all the children of Israel returned, every man to his possession, into their own cities.

Total destruction of the terms token and targets of such covenant cleanses the life, family and community and brings about restoration and prosperity in every area. Please do it today.

Matt 18:18

Verily I say unto you, Whatsoever ye shall bind on earth shall be bound in heaven: and whatsoever ye shall loose on earth shall be loosed in heaven.

Your willingness to surrender every item connected to the satanic covenant for destruction by the anointed servant of God breaks the link and close the door way. Every medium, object, sign, seal, symbol, documents, certificate of initiation (if any), demonic rings and amulets, mirror, plates, pots, oil and shrines, trees and altars, must be destroyed, animals, clothes or membership uniforms, other dresses, cosmetics, must be brought for destruction. These are tokens and they open the doorway.

(Deuteronomy 7 vs. 5)

Acts 19:18-19

And many that believed came, and confessed, and shewed their deeds. Many of them also which used curious arts brought their books together, and burned them before all men: and they counted the price of them, and found it fifty thousand pieces of silver.

As you step out, don't look back, you are being backed up by the spirit of God.

Isa 41:10

Fear thou not; for I am with thee: be not dismayed; for I am thy God: I will strengthen thee; yea, I will help thee; yea, I will uphold thee with the right hand of my righteousness.

This is God encouraging and strengthening you to go ahead that nothing shall by any means hurt you.

Luke 10:19

Behold, I give unto you power to tread on serpents and scorpions, and over all the power of the enemy: and nothing shall by any means hurt you.

If you do it right and sincere, God will be delighted to use you for his glory.

2 Tim 2:21

If a man therefore purge himself from these, he shall be a vessel unto honour, sanctified, and meet for the master's use, and prepared unto every good work.

CHAPTER TEN

MAKING A NEW COVENANT WITH GOD

A successful covenant breaking with the kingdom of darkness should lead to a successful covenant establishment with God to close the gap and make a superior replacement of power and authority over your life.

> *Heb 8:7-8*

> *For if that first covenant had been faultless, then should no place have been sought for the second. For finding fault with them, he saith, Behold, the days come, saith the Lord, when I will make a new covenant with the house of Israel and with the house of Judah:*

A faulty covenant when broken must be replaced with a right one. God's covenant when entered and observed the principles brings blessing, honour and longevity of life. God's covenant is founded on the blood of Jesus which speaks better things and the promises are reliable and the fulfillment is possible.

Heb 12:24

And to Jesus the mediator of the new covenant, and to the blood of sprinkling, that speaketh better things than that of Abel.

The blood of the finished work on Calvary seals the new covenant and Jesus himself is a mediator. A mediator is a meddle person between two parties. At this point, he links us back to the father and bridge the gap of enmity between us and God, reconciling us to God in the cross of his death. His blood satisfied the fathers demand, settled every debt we owed, settled every curse we carried, cleanses us from all unrighteous deeds and restores us back to our position. He pleads our cause before the father, because he sits on the mercy seat interceding for us. We must receive Him as our LORD and SAVIOUR, master and king over our souls.

Heb 9:15-16

And for this cause he is the mediator of the new testament, that by means of death, for the redemption of the transgressions that were under the first testament, they which are called might receive the promise of eternal inheritance. For where a testament is, there must also of necessity be the death of the testator.

20,22

Saying, This is the blood of the testament which God hath enjoined unto you.

And almost all things are by the law purged with blood; and without shedding of blood is no remission.

Under the dispensation of grace, only the blood of Jesus is solemnly required for the establishment of a covenant with God. He has founded the new covenant with the blood by his death. A testator must necessarily die to enforce the strength of such covenant.

This new covenant on the blood of Jesus is founded on better promises. Better and eternal life, successful marriage life, business break-even, fruitfulness, and life actualization in every functional area. This blood takes us to the place we have lost through Adamic sins and positions us as sons and co-heirs to the eternal live in heaven. It makes the blessings God promised to Abraham to be ours in Christ.

> *Gal 3:13-14*
>
> *Christ hath redeemed us from the curse of the law, being made a curse for us: for it is written, Cursed is every one that hangeth on a tree: That the blessing of Abraham might come on the Gentiles through Jesus Christ; that we might receive the promise of the Spirit through faith.*
>
> *Gen 17:1-2*
>
> *And when Abram was ninety years old and nine, the Lord appeared to Abram, and said unto him, I am the Almighty God; walk before me, and be thou perfect. And I will make my covenant between me and thee, and will multiply thee exceedingly.*

God's requirement for this covenant with him is righteousness, perfection and sanctification, once we are able to fulfill these principle requirements, his covenant brings blessing, multiplication, fruitfulness and enjoyments.

It raises us from slavery to the position of a price, father and king.

Gen 17:4

As for me, behold, my covenant is with thee, and thou shalt be a father of many nations.

6-8

And I will make thee exceeding fruitful, and I will make nations of thee, and kings shall come out of thee. And I will establish my covenant between me and thee and thy seed after thee in their generations for an everlasting covenant, to be a God unto thee, and to thy seed after thee. And I will give unto thee, and to thy seed after thee, the land wherein thou art a stranger, all the land of Canaan, for an everlasting possession; and I will be their God.

These are numerous blessings God promised to Abraham as the covenant is made and established. It pays to be in covenant relationship with God, so many benefits are involved. As you acknowledge Jesus as the Lord of your life and accept by cleansing the power of his blood, your victory is guaranteed.

Rev 12:11

And they overcame him by the blood of the Lamb, and by the word of their testimony; and they loved not their lives unto the death.

The testimony is that it is finished; Jesus paid it all and paid it in full. Step out for your rights.

LOOSE HIM AND LET HIM GO

Let us move into the realm of the spirit with strong declarations in prayer to loose and set the captives free. Please be serious at this point of prophetic declarations, and all chains shall be broken in Jesus name.

James 1:25

But whoso looketh into the perfect law of liberty, and continueth therein, he being not a forgetful hearer, but a doer of the work, this man shall be blessed in his deed.

Heb 8:13

In that he saith, A new covenant, he hath made the first old. Now that which decayeth and waxeth old is ready to vanish away.

I stand in the authority of the word of God and the blood of Jesus to declare, that every covenant that was entered against me by my forbearers, parents, or whoever knowingly or unknowingly to me I declare such covenant broken in the name of Jesus. Every term of covenant and their token from me physically or spiritually to establish satanic covenant against my marriage, childbearing, health, finances, or whatever spirit assigned to fight by life destiny and fortune, I command them broken and cast out in Jesus name. I frustrate the token and term of such demonic covenant, over my soul, spirit and body in Jesus name. I use the blood of Jesus as a price to pay and buy backs my soul or family from all demonic realms in Jesus name.

Everything I said yes to which is contrary to the purpose of God concerning me, I say no to it in Jesus name. I command my soul out of witchcraft coven, I announce my soul free from every soul tie to any satanic agents or demons in Jesus name. I invoke my soul using the blood of Jesus as the final sacrifice from any realm of demonic activity in Jesus name. Every demonic deposit inside of me as, sickness, demonic doorway, blood, and demonic food in dream or whatever destroyed in Jesus name. I summon every ancestral spirits of the family living or dead to release everything that belong to me in Jesus name.

I announce my soul transfer from the kingdom of darkness into the kingdom of God through the vehicle of the Holy Spirit in Jesus name. I declare a change of demonic dreams and visions forthwith and a release of angelic coverage over my soul, family and community in Jesus name. I declare every hand writing of satanic ordinances against me erased with the blood of Jesus. I sprinkle the blood of Jesus over myself, family and community, I frustrate every token used in the past, present or future against me in Jesus name. I settle my family living or dead with the blood of Jesus any claim they want to make on my life in Jesus name.

I merge my repented and sanctified soul in the ocean of the blood of Jesus for cleansing and regeneration of life in Jesus name. I invoke the intercessory prayer Jesus made in gospel John 17:5-9 to begin to manifest in my life in Jesus name. I open the exit of my life and command a flush and a purge of all the negative content of my life in Jesus name.

I sanctify my soul and declare that every old covenant of bondage, affliction and desolation broken in Jesus name. Anything that belongs to me in the water, forest, cemetery, covens, in the realm of evil spirits and ancestral altars to disappear immediately in Jesus name.

All satanic marks on me, symbols of identity disappear in Jesus name. I initiate my soul into a new covenant with Jesus through his blood and officially announce it in all realms in Jesus name. I am presented by the angel of the Lord to the Almighty God for a new covenant name which is not known to my family in Jesus name. I finally receive baptism in the realm of the spirit into the family of God and receive the mark of the Lord Jesus. I therefore stand justified before God unto the end of my life in Jesus name. This new covenant with the Lord is signed and sealed today… Put the date when you read to the end in Jesus name. If the son sets you free you are free indeed, Amen.

Lightning Source UK Ltd.
Milton Keynes UK
UKOW02n1437131016

285210UK00002B/10/P